Special Praise for
Behind the Therapy Door

"*Behind the Therapy Door* shares the stories of women whose lives are transformed as they commit to seeking greater truth and awareness. Randy Kamen has a beautiful way of guiding these woman, who represent a piece of us all, to discover their own capacity to move through challenges with courage, vulnerability, and wholeheartedness. The mind-body practices she utilizes help create a heightened state of calm, clarity, connectedness and ultimately, wisdom. Best of all, this book offers a systematic approach that can benefit everyone who wants to deepen their own personal journey and clarify their vision for next steps."

Joan Borysenko, PhD
Founding Partner, Mind-Body Health Sciences, LLC
Bestselling author of *Minding the Body, Mending the Mind*

"I have been a practicing therapist for thirty years and still learned a tremendous amount from reading *Behind the Therapy Door*. Randy Kamen provides clinical insight, compassion, and empathy, as well as a focus on the acquisition of terrific life-affirming skills. Any woman who reads this book will gain a newfound ability to enjoy her life more, and to appreciate what life brings her in the future."

Alice D. Domar, PhD
Executive Director, Domar Center for Mind/Body Health
and Associate Professor at Harvard Medical School

"*Behind the Therapy Door* offers what we all yearn for: clear, applicable guidance for concerns that are deep-rooted and complicated. Dr. Kamen provides wise counsel for women for those moments when we become lost in emotions, thoughts, or behaviors that cause harm to our own psyche and those we love. Her guidance, rooted in science and decades of experience, is both a light and a path, providing exactly what we need when we are overwhelmed by fear, sorrow, anxiety, or shame. The articulation of exercises, such as breath meditation and affirmations, gives us the tools to become calmer, clearer, healthier, and wiser—even in moments of great distress. I applaud Dr. Kamen for the tremendous effort and discernment that is required to make complicated understandings simple. This is a book I will send to many and am thrilled to be able to do so."

Maria Sirois, PsyD
Author of *A Short Course in Happiness After Loss (and Other Dark, Difficult Times)* and *Every Day Counts*

"In *Behind the Therapy Door*, Randy Kamen invites you into the intimacy of her office and into the stories of her clients. These courageous women face the loss, challenges, and pain that are familiar to us all in one way or another. As you learn the tools and strategies Dr. Kamen uses to help them move toward healing and wholeness, you can experience a greater sense of hope and empowerment. This important book details an evidenced-based systematic approach that elevates women to the next phase of their lives with greater calm, clarity, and courage. Let Dr. Kamen guide you in your own journey to find greater joy, connection and meaning."

Loretta LaRoche
Founder and President, The Humor Potential, Inc.
Author of *Life Is Short, Wear Your Party Pants* and
Relax—You May Only Have a Few Minutes Left: Using the Power of Humor to Overcome Stress in Your Life and Work

"Tender, loving, wise, smart, and above all useful, *Behind the Therapy Door* answers most of the important questions regarding big emotions, from love to guilt to grief to feeling bad about yourself. Combining decades of experience as a therapist with a practical mind and a huge heart, Randy Kamen has written a phenomenally helpful book. I could not recommend it more highly."

Edward Hallowell, MD
Author of *Driven to Distraction: Recognizing and Coping with Attention Deficit Disorder from Childhood through Adulthood,* and *Connect: 12 Vital Ties That Open Your Heart, Lengthen Your Life, and Deepen Your Soul*

"There is a power in the sharing of real-life journeys of struggle that can heal your heart and soul like no other. Couple it with outstanding therapeutic guidance and proven, practical strategies and you have everything you need to navigate obstacles and scale your own mountains. I love everything about this book!"

Debbie Phillips
Founder, Women on Fire®, author, *Women on Fire: 21 Inspiring Women Share Their Life Secrets (and Save You Years of Struggle!)*

BEHIND THE THERAPY DOOR

BEHIND THE THERAPY DOOR

Simple Strategies to Transform Your Life

Randy Kamen

CENTRAL RECOVERY PRESS

LAS VEGAS

Central Recovery Press (CRP) is committed to publishing exceptional materials addressing addiction treatment, recovery, and behavioral healthcare topics, including original and quality books, audio/visual communications, and web-based new media. Through a diverse selection of titles, we seek to contribute a broad range of unique resources for professionals, recovering individuals and their families, and the general public.

For more information, visit www.centralrecoverypress.com.

Publisher: Central Recovery Press
      3321 N. Buffalo Drive
      Las Vegas, NV 89129

22 21 20 19 18 17   1 2 3 4 5

Library of Congress Cataloging-in-Publication Data
Names: Kamen, Randy, author.
Title: Behind the therapy door : simple strategies to transform your life /
Randy Kamen, EdD.
Description: Las Vegas : Central Recovery Press, [2017]
Identifiers: LCCN 2017007552 (print) | LCCN 2017009158 (ebook) | ISBN
9781942094418 (paperback) | ISBN 9781942094425
Subjects: LCSH: Psychotherapy. | Mind and body. | Psychotherapist and
patient. | BISAC: PSYCHOLOGY / Emotions. | SELF-HELP / Personal Growth /
Self-Esteem. | SELF-HELP / Personal Growth / General. | PSYCHOLOGY /
Psychotherapy / Counseling.
Classification: LCC RC475 .K36 2017 (print) | LCC RC475 (ebook) | DDC
616.89/14--dc23
LC record available at https://lccn.loc.gov/2017007552

Photo of Randy Kamen by Janet Wolbarst Photography. Used with permission.

Every attempt has been made to contact copyright holders. If copyright holders have not been properly acknowledged, please contact us. Central Recovery Press will be happy to rectify the omission in future printings of this book.

Publisher's Note: This book contains general information about the process of psychotherapy, as well as practices that can promote learning, growth, and healing. The information is not medical advice and should not be treated as such. Central Recovery Press makes no representations or warranties in relation to the information in this book. If you have specific questions about any medical matter discussed in this book, you should consult your doctor or other professional healthcare provider. This book is not an alternative to medical advice from your doctor or other professional healthcare provider.

Our books represent the experiences and opinions of their authors only. Every effort has been made to ensure that events, institutions, and statistics presented in our books as facts are accurate and up-to-date. To protect their privacy, the names of some of the people, places, and institutions in this book have been changed.

Author's Note: *Behind the Therapy Door* was inspired by the stories of many women. Each woman presented is fictitious. Names, characters, places, and incidents are either the composites of several women's stories, products of the author's imagination, or used fictitiously. Any resemblance to actual events or locales or persons, living or dead, is entirely coincidental. The strategies and skills illustrated within this book are not meant for use in lieu of medical or psychological intervention.

Cover design by The Book Designers
Interior design by Six Penny Graphics

To my beloved Martin, Amy, and Max

Table of Contents

Acknowledgments

My deepest gratitude to Martin, my loving and supportive husband, who spent countless hours reading, editing, and thinking through ideas with me, and to my Amy and Max, who have taught me my most important lessons about love, parenting, and being my best possible self.

To my dear friend, colleague, and insightful reader, Holly Friedman Glick, LICSW, RYT.

To Jeanne Fredericks, my agent, who believed in the worthiness of this project in its infancy.

To Dan Mager, my editor at Central Recovery Press, whose thoughtful conversations and edits brought this book to its latest and most comprehensive iteration.

To my family, teachers, editors, and friends, whose support made my life sweeter and my work more meaningful, and who helped me bring this book to life: Julie Silver, MD; Virginia LaPlante; Lesley Ehlers; Edie Ravanelle; Sherry Sidoti, RYT; Pamela Romanow; Jill Karp; Cantor Hollis Schachner; Derry Schwantner; Liza Burkin; Lee Rosenbaum, MD; Jane Murphy; Susan Aiello; Lisa Tener; Maureen Strafford, MD; Robin Schoenthaler, MD; David Doolittle, PsyD; Alan Bergstein; Robert Berkley; Jodi Raphael; Dena Judah; Caryl Shaw; Ronni Simon; Peter Simon; Carole Osterer; Lauren Rikleen; Nancy Bergstein; Dianne Silvestri, MD; Susanna Brougham; Cheryl Savit; Ellen Sard; Sandy Jaffe; Susan Benjamin; Janet Wolbarst; Jodi Swartz; Jenna Keith; Sharon Kamen; and Kooper.

Great appreciation and gratitude go out to my patients and students, who have allowed me into their lives and had the courage to look within and share from the deepest place in their hearts.

CHAPTER ONE

Open the Door to Your Best Self

*B*ehind the Therapy Door: Simple Strategies to Transform Your Life takes you on a journey into the inner sanctum of a psychologist's office. From this unique vantage point, you will hear the intimate conversations between therapist and client, witness firsthand the benefits of mind and body strategies, and gain insight from the experiences of six women in the throes of transition. Their treatment within the therapy setting becomes your springboard for learning important life lessons. You will acquire tools and strategies that will help you develop more loving and sustainable relationships, and lead you to your best possible life.

As a psychologist and educator for over thirty-five years, I have listened to a multitude of women who discount their own value and fail to step into their personal power. They talk about feeling disconnected, unhappy, and unable to move forward with their lives. Yet when these same women are equipped with tools to nurture themselves and build stronger relationships and support systems, their feelings of alienation subside, and their lives begin to flourish.

The Framework for *Behind the Therapy Door*

I chose to use stories and the patient-therapist dialogue as the primary framework for this book. All human beings, particularly women, love stories. They help us make sense of our world and our experience in it. Stories create comfort and connection. Whether with friends, family, a therapist, or a group, women find it healing to talk about their emotional realities. When we are feeling supported, our physical, emotional, and social lives are enriched, and we gain the fortitude needed for times of challenge and transition.

Behind the Therapy Door tells the stories of women whose search to find greater meaning and love paves the way for readers to do the same. Each story depicts the common challenges associated with loss, loneliness, and alienation, and speaks to the desire we all share to create a full and gratifying life. By sharing their stories and integrating mindfulness and relational skills, these women overcome personal battles and find greater peace. Over time, each woman learns mind-body strategies that expand her capacity to tolerate painful emotions and create more loving relationships.

Emotional Set Point

Every person has a natural set point for feeling states, like a thermostat. Genetics, upbringing, and personality play important roles in determining where this set point lies. Some people tend to be more naturally optimistic, while others see life through a more negative lens. Life events sway the thermostat, but in most cases we return to our familiar set point. The practices delineated in *Behind the Therapy Door* show how to positively alter the brain's chemistry and consequently boost this set point in healthy and lasting ways.

This ability to modify our "emotional thermostat" is a breakthrough in the field of psychology. In this book, the methods that help alter brain chemistry are presented in small, consumable bites that build upon each other.

Mind-Body Strategies and Contemporary Science

Mind-body strategies and ancient contemplative practices have become integrated into contemporary psychology and medicine. For example, learning to elicit a relaxation response through abdominal breathing, relaxation training, yoga, or prayer helps us become less susceptible to the negative effects of stress and improves our health, happiness, and productivity. It has been shown that abdominal breathing quiets the mind and calms the nervous system. Abdominal breathing builds the capacity to think with clarity and in the moment, rather than simply operating on automatic pilot.

By learning a simple meditation technique, we become aware of ourselves from the inside out. We bear witness to our internal experiences and do not simply react to thoughts and sensations as they arise. Meditation helps to manage stress, anxiety, depression, pain, loss, and compulsive behaviors. It also improves concentration, cognitive function, insight, intuition, creativity, and wisdom.

Modern science teaches us that our brains are malleable, or "neuroplastic." This refers to the brain's ability to reshape or reorganize itself by forming new neural connections as a result of our experiences. We can "train our brains" to be calm, optimistic, and compassionate. Self-hypnosis and visualization methods help to minimize negative thoughts and emotions while building and expanding a repertoire of positive thoughts and actions. With practice, we can learn to savor positive experiences so they become deeply embedded in our minds, bodies, and hearts.

Positive Psychology and Mind-Body Connection

The growing interest in the mind-body connection parallels the study and practice of "positive psychology." Rather than focusing on mental illness, positive psychologists seek to cultivate the individual's unique abilities and make everyday life more fulfilling. With positive psychology tools, people can build more positive emotions, amplify their strengths, and tune into their highest purpose.

Qualities like altruism, spirituality, creativity, courage, gratitude, wisdom, and the capacity to love and be loved can be gleaned through the stories in this book. You will notice that when the women in these stories combine their personal strengths and abilities with insight and mindfulness strategies, they begin to achieve greater joy and fulfillment, even in the face of loss and disappointment.

Women and Friendship

As human beings, we are all social creatures and we need strong, positive relationships to thrive. Those with robust social ties have fewer medical or psychological problems and recover faster from trauma and illness. Women have been shown to be hardwired for friendship.[1] We have a powerful biological need to connect with each other, which is demonstrated by surges in our hormones when we gather. Friendships increase our sense of belonging and purpose and improve mood and self-esteem. Research shows that women with close friends live longer, happier, and more fulfilling lives.

According to Harvard Health Publications, social connections buffer us from many of the harmful effects of stress, which can impair the arteries of the heart, the immune system, gut function, and insulin regulation.[2] Friendships help protect us from disease, decrease our perception of pain, and motivate us to recover from illnesses and injuries. These vital social ties also make life passages such as aging, divorce, trauma, job loss, and death of a loved one more tolerable.

In this multitasking, techno-crazed life, many people have forgotten the simple pleasures of being present with friends. Bringing the mindful, grounded self into the context of healthy friendships helps us to heal our wounds, nourish our souls, and strengthen our resiliency. Those nurtured by friendships have more positive energy for themselves, as well as for others whose lives they touch. *Behind the Therapy Door* is about finding happiness and purpose and cultivating loving relationships, so that no matter what challenges life sends our way we feel able to carry on.

Mind-body medicine, mindfulness, and positive psychology strategies lay the foundation for highly effective self-care and a strong inner core. When we center ourselves, we are poised to realize our potential, build healthy relationships, and make a positive difference in the lives of others.

---

[1] http://www.anapsid.org/cnd/gender/tendfend.html (accessed January 4, 2017).

[2] http://www.health.harvard.edu/newsletter_article/the-health-benefits-of-strong-relationships (accessed January 4, 2017).

The Impetus for *Behind the Therapy Door*

Several years ago, after attending the Massachusetts Conference for Women, I discovered that even as women have become more educated, financially independent, and competitive in the workforce, they have become increasingly unhappy. This downward trend is influenced by the stress created by the contemporary demands of the workplace, which have been layered upon the more traditional responsibilities of home and hearth. In combination with a greater sense of social isolation, these realities have generated distress and unhappiness for considerable numbers of women.

Many women have become detached from friends, neighbors, and families. When connections deteriorate, personal and communal lives suffer, as do physical and emotional health. Ironically, with advancements in information and communication technologies there seems to be even less time to reconcile the competing obligations of work, family, and self-care. Sadly, women tend to feel the resulting stress more acutely than men.

My intention in writing this book is to help more women become unwilling to settle for low self-esteem and unhappiness, and to empower them with strategies that foster greater inner strength and resilience. My wish is to help you answer the question poised so wonderfully by Pulitzer Prize–winning author Mary Oliver in her poem "The Summer Day." She writes, "Tell me, what is it you plan to do with your one wild and precious life?"

The Mission for *Behind the Therapy Door*

What do I really want out of my life, and how can I make it happen? How do I realize my deepest dreams and desires? How can I make a difference in the lives of others? The answers to these questions are more accessible than you might imagine. Through the wisdom found in these compelling stories, this book is designed to help you get unstuck, achieve your goals, and transform your relationships.

My hope is that the benefits derived from internalizing tools presented in *Behind the Therapy Door* will be life altering and, in certain instances, lifesaving. Learn from the universal struggles experienced by these six women and customize the strategies offered to address your personal needs. I encourage you to embrace and practice these techniques until they are integrated into your everyday life. You may begin to notice your own personal metamorphosis.

Consider keeping this practical guide accessible, referencing it often to review the strategies presented. These are tools that, with regular practice, will change your life in a lasting way. I encourage you to augment the knowledge you gain here with the online support I provide through webinars, online courses, podcasts, and other social media venues available on my website at www.DrRandyKamen.com.

CHAPTER TWO
Grappling with Old Demons

Anne

Anne came to see me seeking a referral for her seventeen-year-old son, Justin. She arrived dressed in a crisp white blouse, a navy-blue skirt, and sensible flats. A waft of cigarette smoke trailed her as she entered my office. Her petite physique looked strong, her posture erect and graceful. She looked young for her mid-forties, although I could detect fine lines in her complexion, likely from years of smoking. She spoke in terse, measured sentences, as if reading from a script, and her pale face was frozen into a polite semi-smile. Ill at ease, she squirmed a bit as she sat down on the edge of my couch.

Anne began by telling me that her once easygoing, spontaneous son now isolated himself in his room. His lethargic, sullen demeanor worried her. When she tried to communicate with Justin, he either ignored her or, more typically, exhibited disgust or anger. He complained about her cooking and snarled whenever she asked about his life. "He spends most of his time alone, listening to music or playing video games in his room, and doesn't seem to have any friends," said Anne. "He relates to his father, Stephen, and his brother, Matthew, who is away at college, but that's it."

Stephen and Anne worked full time, Stephen as a freelance photographer and Anne as a middle school English teacher. "We're both worried about Justin's withdrawal and isolation. I'm really concerned that he's depressed and might be thinking of hurting himself."

When I asked her to elaborate, Anne, face flushed, said that she didn't think Justin was in immediate danger, but she wanted me to see him soon. I agreed to meet with Justin a few days later. I also asked Anne to meet with me weekly for a few sessions, so I could learn more about the family dynamics and discuss some effective ways for her to improve her communication with her son.

Although she agreed, Anne made a point of telling me she wanted to keep her own history private. I said I would respect her request. I wondered what had happened in Anne's own life that she could not allow to be spoken. Perhaps she had suffered some earlier trauma and only now, when her son's emotional well-being seemed in jeopardy, was she willing to seek help. I hoped that eventually Anne would feel more comfortable sharing her own story.

Meeting Justin

As planned, I met with Justin for an initial assessment. His slouched and rounded shoulders did nothing to diminish a tall, lanky frame that sported a faded T-shirt and baggy jeans that rode precariously below his hips. Without a belt, he might have been in serious trouble! Cell phone in hand, Justin gave me a sideways glance and took a seat, his dirty blond bangs almost completely covering his sad eyes.

Much to my surprise, he began to speak candidly about school, his lack of friends, and his miserable relationship with his mother. He struck me as a warm, intelligent, engaging young man with low self-esteem and mild depression. Justin loathed high school and felt rejected by the other kids. Although he used to get invited to some weekend social activities, the invitations had dwindled and now ceased altogether, so he spent his free time in his room getting lost in music, books, and video games. He was embarrassed that his only real friend was his father, although he loved their shared passion for music and photography. In short order, he let me know what was *really* bothering him at home.

"I know I have issues, but my mom is the sick one. She is obsessive, weird, and afraid of her shadow. She comes home from work, cooks, cleans, and smokes the night away, reading her books or watching her shows. She holds me back from doing anything fun. I can't wait to get out of the house. My brother is so happy being away at college. He hardly ever comes home. Now I'm the only one home and the singular target of her craziness."

Justin seemed perceptive and self-aware. He understood that he was struggling socially, but he didn't appear to be self-destructive and, paradoxically, was worried about his mother's well-being. He continued, "I don't know if my mom told you, but my grandmother died about a year ago. I didn't really know her, but it's definitely taken a toll on my mom. It's made her paranoid and her moods way worse."

Anne was mourning the loss of her mother, which I suspected was complicated and among the private pieces of personal information she did not want to share. I asked Justin how the loss had affected him. "It's sad, I guess, but I'm okay. My mom, on the other hand, seems to be getting more negative and stressed. Until my grandmother died, she hadn't seen or spoken to her sisters in more than a decade. As far as I'm concerned, she needs therapy more than me. The truth is, I worry about both my parents. Neither of them takes good care of themselves. Not only does my mother chain-smoke, but she hardly eats. I don't know if she has anorexia, but to me she looks scary thin. My father lives on junk food, never works out, has a big gut, and both of them have no friends." Justin's worry seemed to have merit. While he was definitely angry at his mother's intrusiveness, he seemed more concerned about the health of his parents.

Bouts of Loneliness

Occasional bouts of loneliness and depression are common and affect most of us at some point. Usually, these episodes are short-lived and occur around periods of transition, such as the loss of a loved one, losing touch with a friend, moving to a new home, or being downsized from a job. While most people are able to move through the difficult feelings associated with life transitions and emerge successfully, some cannot. This is especially true when the transitions are layered upon previous trauma that is not yet sufficiently resolved. Many people find they can benefit from professional support and coping strategies to overcome their dark periods and learn to live their best possible lives.

In my many years of working with patients, I have repeatedly observed that most emotional suffering comes from worrying about the future or ruminating about something from the past. In Anne's case, unfounded or not, she was worried that her son's depression might lead him to harm himself. The more she worried and expressed her concerns, the more she alienated him. Although I still did not know the source of her pain, according to Justin's clues and her own unusually emphatic request for privacy, she was clearly troubled about something. Anne's method of self-protection was to isolate from friends and family, just as she planned to keep the therapeutic relationship with me at arm's length. The question was, "Self-protection from what?"

Justin continued, "I know my mother worries I might be suicidal, but I promise, I'm not. I just want friends. I don't have anyone to hang with anymore. I'm burned out on the stoners, and the nerdy group is too weird for me. I just need to get out of this provincial little town and find my way, without my mother hovering over me, trying to control my every move. My grades haven't been great this semester, but I think I'll get into a decent college. I do want help finding some kind of support group, as dorky as that sounds." He rolled his eyes and sighed. "The truth is I could definitely use a few friends, but please do what you can to help my mother. She's the scary one, not me."

Justin's assessment of the situation struck me as astute. He knew he needed some specific help with his current social situation, whereas his mother was the one hiding from her own pain. I assured Justin that I would do my best, but his mom needed to make the decision to let me in. I promised to remain available to him as a resource, but suggested that he meet with a male colleague who could offer him an adolescent group to help with his social isolation. He agreed.

The First Session

Anne was scheduled for her first session with me later that week. When she came in, she informed me, "I am willing to talk about anything that would help Justin. I might need guidance along the way, but as I told you, I do not want to dig deeply into my own past." Her guard was up, posture rigid, movements controlled, and there was a measured quality to her speech. Anne shared Justin's developmental history.

Justin had been an easy delivery, arriving the week of his due date. A healthy, gregarious baby, he had worshipped his older brother from the time he could toddle around after him. Most of the time, they had played well together. He'd also had a little group of friends who would come over periodically for play dates, and he always had a couple of good buddies. Around Justin's seventh birthday, he began to develop a passion for reading autobiographies and history books. Anne had taken great pleasure in reading Justin's compositions, as had his teachers. According to Anne, Justin had always been a good boy without any behavioral worries, until he began withdrawing in high school.

Through several conversations, we slowly established a rapport, but Anne remained tight-lipped when it came to discussing her own past. I waited cautiously for an opportunity to dig deeper. About a month into our sessions, Anne said, "I've been noticing how much Justin isolates himself from the outside world and how it's taking a toll. It makes me realize that I do the same. My whole life revolves around my family and work. I never speak with anyone about personal matters. I was taught that family loyalty and privacy were to be upheld at all costs. Even Stephen doesn't know details of my whole story. I don't think the secrecy has served me well over the years, but it is all that I ever knew. Justin gets that from me."

She looked at me directly, as though she had just had some sort of profound revelation, and then rapidly continued: "There's something else you need to know. My sister Beth committed suicide about thirty years ago. She hanged herself in the basement. By the time she was found, she was gone. I'm terrified that Justin might be entertaining such thoughts. I've never spoken to anyone but Stephen about Beth's death, but I thought you should know. It was all too hideous, and besides, my mother insisted that we never speak about Beth with outsiders."

The Dark Side of Stress

There it was! Anne had entered therapy, reluctantly, to help her son. During our first few sessions, she was able to access the tip of her own personal iceberg of pain—and the stress of keeping it in check—that had permeated every aspect of her life and her relationships.

Stress of any sort is so commonplace that it often can feel normal, even in the midst of abnormal or tragic circumstances, such as the suicide of a sibling. It becomes the only way of life we know. This is especially true as we move from a childhood trauma into a busy adult life, juggling family and work responsibilities. As a young working mom, Anne had focused completely on creating a good life for her family. But as her children grew, she found herself feeling more afraid and withdrawn. The longer she isolated herself from others and kept her past a secret, the more scared and stressed she became. Although Anne believed that her son was the one at risk of harming himself, it is not unusual to see in others that which we find difficult to recognize and acknowledge in ourselves. I wondered whether her concern was a projection of her own self-destructive choices.

When we are constantly stressed and operating in "emergency mode"—as Anne was when she vigilantly guarded her family history and the secret of her sister's suicide—the mind and body pay a steep price. The ability to think clearly and to feel our best can become seriously impaired. The scientist Hans Selye coined the term *stress* in 1936. He defined it as the "nonspecific response of the body to any demand for change." It matters not whether the demand is real or perceived. As he explained in *Stress without Distress* in 1974, "It is not stress that kills us, it is our reaction to it."[3]

Misperceived or mismanaged stress can make us unhappy and sick with physical symptoms such as sleep disturbances, fatigue, pain, high blood pressure, heart palpitations, weight gain or loss, and digestive problems. Some common psychological manifestations of stress include anxiety, irritability, depression, memory lapses, poor concentration, phobias, and feeling out of control.

Managing stress and trauma often begins with the willingness to self-disclose, or share, our personal story. This is the first step toward making sense of our complicated emotional realities. Like Anne, sometimes patients do not come right out and tell me what the problem is. Instead,

[3] Hans Selye, *Stress Without Distress* (Philadelphia, PA: Lippincott Williams & Wilkins, 1974).

they talk about someone or something else to stay away from the pain of their own old wounds. It takes time to trust, to find a safe haven in which we can reveal our stories and gain a deeper understanding of the disappointments and hurts we have experienced.

After years of silence, in the name of helping her son, Anne decided to let someone other than her husband know that there had been a family suicide. Immediately after sharing that information, Anne straightened up and said in a restrained cadence, "I've told you the important information, now I just want to make sure that my boy is safe." As rapidly as Anne had opened up, she shut down any further discussion.

Reluctant to let her shut down, I offered, "Your loyalty to your family and the secrecy you maintained may have protected you from the pain over the years, but these days it seems to be interfering with getting you the help you need. You might find sharing your story to be both cathartic and instructive. You and Stephen have been good parents, and despite Justin having some issues now, he seems to be headed in the right direction. Maybe this is a good time for you to consider getting help for yourself and come to terms with some of the events from your past."

Anne said she would think about this. Several days before our next scheduled meeting, she called me, sounding frantic. She had been hospitalized over the weekend for chest pain and shortness of breath. Other than slightly elevated blood pressure, Anne's lab results did not reveal anything. She had been told that her symptoms were consistent with severe anxiety or a panic attack.

Anxiety and Depression

Anxiety and depression are the hallmark feelings that bring people into therapy. They often mask deeper emotions that we wish to avoid or dare not feel, such as anger, shame, fear, or guilt. Depression occurs when we suppress and become numb to our feelings, whereas anxiety occurs when we take flight from our feelings or enter a heightened state of "fight-or-flight" arousal. Either way, we avoid authentic feelings that unconsciously seem to be more than we can tolerate. When we allow ourselves to observe, explore, experience, and finally resolve these feelings, only then are we liberated to move forward in our lives in a healthier way.

Anne arrived at my office later that day, hands trembling as she handed me her hospital report: "I felt like I was having a heart attack. I just can't bear the thought of dying and leaving Stephen and the kids." She huddled on my couch, wrapped her arms around her thin body, and waited for my response.

"Thankfully, that is not what's going on," I reassured her, while scanning her medical record. "Your report indicates high blood pressure, which can be managed through medication and making some lifestyle changes. For example, learning some breathing and meditation techniques and getting more exercise will help considerably. I would be happy to show you some relaxation skills right now that you can learn quickly. Other than that, you seem to be in good health. Panic attacks are terrifying, but they are not life-threatening."

As I assured Anne, there are well-researched and effective strategies that can be incorporated into everyday life to protect us against the deleterious effects of panic, anxiety, and garden-variety stress. These methods also help quiet the mind so we can savor more of life's moment-to-moment experiences. I wanted to teach Anne some simple yet powerful techniques that she could readily incorporate into her busy life.

I also wanted to introduce the idea that physical symptoms can indicate emotional stress and inner turmoil. Anne seemed unaware of this connection and saw her high blood pressure as a strictly medical problem. I told her, "Sometimes bringing up the past, or even thinking about the past, uncovers long-buried feelings that result in anxiety symptoms. It's normal to feel tense or scared when you delve into a painful past. Anxiety is the body's natural response to danger, real or imagined, current or past. My guess is that our last conversation about your sister brought up a traumatic and difficult memory that ignited your panic attack."

When anxiety becomes extreme or constant, it can take a significant toll on health and well-being. Sometimes, as in Anne's case, severe anxiety or panic mimics a heart attack. Typically, medication is used to alleviate the initial symptoms associated with a panic attack, such as a racing heartbeat, weakness, faintness or dizziness, sense of terror or impending doom, sweating, chills, chest pains, breathing difficulties, and feeling a loss of control. Psychotherapy, cognitive behavioral therapy

(CBT), relaxation, and meditation techniques have been shown to be highly effective and preferable over the long term in helping patients control or overcome these symptoms. These methods also enable patients to replace irrational, maladaptive, and self-defeating thoughts with more positive, realistic ones.

I now understood more about Anne's difficult childhood, yet kept wondering what else she was not revealing as she maintained the family code of silence. I decided to bide my time and focus on teaching Anne skills that would help her to control the physical and emotional symptoms that had brought her to the emergency room. I told her, "Learning skills and strategies for improving your resilience and mindfulness will help you calm down and take control before the anxiety becomes overwhelming. You will be better able to prevent future anxiety attacks and minimize the impact of the ones that might break through. Perhaps, after you learn some skills, you will also feel able to speak more openly about your past."

Although recollecting a difficult past may exacerbate emotions initially, when we share our stories with someone we trust, over time it is possible to feel calmer and more at peace. Everyone faces anxiety and intensified emotions at times, but it is important to remember that even the most powerful feelings reach a peak and then subside, like an arc or a wave. We need to learn to "ride the wave" of our emotions, with the understanding that they will eventually level off. Consciously deepening one's breathing when emotions run high fosters the ability to tolerate strong feelings.

Learning to "Tolerate the Affect"

Learning to tolerate the affect means learning to bear and manage intense emotions as they arise. Another way of thinking about this is to cultivate the ability to feel strong emotions or sensations as they present themselves—as we experience them. To do so, begin to observe your feelings without doing anything about them. Try not to judge them or react. Simply notice and perhaps become curious about each feeling state as it comes and goes. As you become aware of your emotions, practice naming each feeling, such as "joy," "anger," or "frustration," in a steady and relaxed way. Then deepen your breath and notice what happens. Perhaps you will sense your emotions building, peaking, or easing and the wave becoming less pronounced. Paying attention to your feelings, rather than simply reacting to them, can reveal much about your inner world and liberate you from the potential storms of emotion and physical sensation.

In contrast, avoiding your feelings delays the process of moving through them successfully. For example, when you numb yourself to the pain of loss or hurt, the associated feelings cannot successfully resolve in your conscious or unconscious mind. Painful feelings, when examined, can become magnified before they quiet down. However, when people allow themselves to observe, feel, and move through their pain, the intensity of their emotions subsides and they gain a greater sense of personal empowerment and resilience.

My goal was to help Anne develop the internal resources needed to allow her complicated and uncomfortable feelings to surface and to learn to tolerate her pain. In this way, she could eventually move beyond the old demons. I knew that if she were able to do this, she would find greater inner peace. Therefore, teaching her a basic approach to use to practice observing and being present with her difficult feelings was an important place to continue our work.

Strategy for Tolerating Painful Feelings

- Notice the feeling as it arises in your mind and body.
- Give it a name, such as anger, sadness, shame, or remorse.
- Take a few deep breaths.
- Observe how the feeling moves through you.
- Remind yourself that you can handle this feeling and that it will subside.
- Pay attention as the feeling begins to pass through and quiet down.

Mindfulness

I explained to Anne that the above technique was not only a way to control her anxiety but also a way to become more mindful, and that increased mindfulness would help her in all facets of her life.

Mindfulness means deliberately paying attention to, and seeing clearly, what is happening in our lives in the present moment, without judgment. It does not eliminate life's stressors, but it can help us respond to them in a calmer manner that also benefits the heart, mind, and body. It helps us to recognize and step away from habitual patterns of behavior, which are often unconscious emotional and physical reactions to everyday events. For example, being mindful helps us make more thoughtful decisions about food, exercise, rest, and perhaps even our relationships.

Our minds have a tendency to wander through all kinds of thoughts and emotions. Some of these are positive, while others may include feelings of unexpressed anger, anxiety, cravings, guilt, and shame. When we indulge ourselves in these negative thoughts, we make them stronger. We do not want to stop thoughts and emotions from entering our minds, as they deepen self-awareness and guide future life choices. Instead, the idea is to notice and observe our feeling states without embellishing them in our minds. It is important to understand that whatever we focus on in our minds becomes stronger. As a result, it behooves us to focus on thoughts that are positive and support our best intentions.

When we pay attention in the present, we are not dwelling in the past or the future. We are anchoring ourselves in the moment, creating a space where peace and contentment can grow and flourish.

Mindfulness also means being consciously nonjudgmental. This gives us a chance to be kinder and more compassionate with ourselves and in our relationships with others. Rather than being judgmental, we can perhaps become more curious about our own behaviors and those of others. We can be aware that an experience, interaction, or feeling is either pleasant or unpleasant, but when we are mindful, we learn to observe rather than judge.

For example, Anne could bring herself into the present moment and be curious about the dynamics with Justin and within herself rather than be critical. This would help her to be more open-minded and positive. Mindfulness is not about creating balance and happiness, although these are often residual benefits. It is about being awake to our lives and finding peace within.

Mindfulness improves our physical and psychological well-being. It heightens our capacity for creativity, intuition, and wisdom. We can train our brains to be more present and less judgmental, to better care for ourselves, to create healthier relationships, and to make better life choices.

The most basic vehicle to mindfulness is the conscious focus on and deepening of the breath through abdominal breathing. From the first time I met Anne, I noticed her breathing was shallow and rapid. I knew that teaching her abdominal breathing so she could learn a simple and effective way to control her anxiety with immediate results would open up Anne to a greater sense of calm and vitality. The regular practice of abdominal breathing and other relaxation techniques are excellent strategies for self-regulating.

Abdominal Breathing

I asked Anne to remember how her children had breathed as babies, their bellies expanding and contracting with each new breath. I said, "Think about the full and rhythmical way in which they breathed. Somewhere along the way, most of us stop doing this and our stress levels increase. When elevated stress levels become consistent, the ongoing state of arousal can begin to seem normal."

Most of us are unaware of the importance of breathing properly and use only a small fraction of our full breathing capacity. Stress, poor posture, long hours in front of a desk or computer, and the wish for a flat stomach promote shallow chest breathing. When we restrict our natural breathing pattern, as we do automatically when we are stressed, the oxygen flow to the brain and body is reduced and we become more anxious. This perpetuates the experience of anxiety and pain within the mind and body.

However, when we deeply expand and contract the breath, oxygenated blood circulates throughout the body and deactivates the autonomic nervous system's stress response. As a result, there is a boost to the immune system, muscles relax, heart rate and blood pressure lower, digestion improves, bone repair and growth occur, and the whole body moves toward a greater state of relaxation. Most important, abdominal breathing evokes a feeling of emotional control along with a sense of mental and physical well-being.

I explained to Anne that abdominal breathing, also known as "belly" or "diaphragmatic" breathing, is the fastest way to change one's physiology, triggering a state of relaxation. I told her, "Relaxation and anxiety are incompatible responses that cannot coexist, because they are two distinct physiological responses. When you practice and internalize the feeling of relaxation, you eventually learn to override the effects of stress and anxiety. Abdominal breathing is the antidote to anxiety and panic."

The method I described was as follows: "Sit in a comfortable position with arms and legs uncrossed. Place one or both hands on the abdomen just below the navel and watch the rise and fall of the low belly. Breathe through the nostrils slowly and deeply. Expand the low belly as you inhale and contract the low belly as you exhale. Allow the exhalation to take twice as long as the inhalation. The relaxation occurs as you breathe out. Practice this for five to ten breaths a session and notice the effects. Abdominal breathing can greatly enhance your breathing capacity. It calms the mind and body and induces a feeling of relaxed attentiveness, which is at the root of mindfulness."

This basic breathing exercise can be practiced anytime you need to relax or to reduce anxiety, stress, or pain. The use of the hands on the chest and abdomen is only needed when you are training yourself to breathe abdominally. Once comfortable with your ability to breathe into the low belly, release the hands and keep them on the lap or to your sides. Go back to using your hands if you want the added reminder to breathe into the belly and keep the chest relatively still.

Anne seemed curious. I told her, "Abdominal breathing requires practice and thought, especially during the initial stages of learning. For now, just watch your breath without changing or manipulating it in any way. Notice the rise and fall of every breath." After a few moments, I asked her what she had observed.

"I don't like this exercise," she responded. "It's making me anxious and self-conscious."

I replied, "Please hang in there with me. It can be frustrating to practice this at first, but I promise it will get easier and feel better if you give it a chance."

Learning abdominal breathing proved to be challenging for Anne because of a lifetime of smoking and her discomfort with these new bodily sensations. Typically, whenever her anxiety kicked in, Anne reached for a cigarette. Now, she needed to train herself to intercept this behavior and learn alternatives for regulating her emotions.

Abdominal, Belly, or Deep-Breathing Strategy

- Sit comfortably with spine supported. Breath flows more freely when the body is aligned.
- Release the low back into the chair, lift up the chest bone, and relax the shoulders.
- Put one hand on your low belly and the other on your chest.
- Inhale through the nostrils and feel the belly expand. The chest hardly moves.
- Exhale and feel the hand on the belly move in.
- Breathe out completely without forcing the breath.
- Take twice as long to exhale as to inhale.
- Practice several times a day or whenever feeling the first signs of stress.

The Three-Part Breath

Anne's breathing remained rapid and shallow over the next few sessions. I suggested she practice the three-part breath so that she had another technique that might be easier to learn. For the three-part breath:

1. Breathe into your low belly.
2. Let the oxygen move into your diaphragm, and then your chest.
3. When you exhale, breathe out from your low belly, diaphragm, and chest.

The three-part breath is deeper than the abdominal breath. It is a good way to begin a meditation or visualization exercise, as it quickly sends a message to the brain to relax mind and body. This breath is not intended for regular use; about five of these breaths are optimal to initiate a relaxation response. I thought it would be good for Anne to feel the immediate physiological effects from this powerful breath.

Unlike abdominal breathing, the three-part breath is not to be used all the time because it involves taking your fullest breath possible. Respiration deepens and lung capacity improves from the practice of this way of breathing.

I instructed Anne to sit comfortably in good posture and place one hand on her heart or upper chest and the other on her low belly. "Relax your shoulders and upper torso," I instructed. "Inhale slowly through the nostrils, feel the low belly expand, then the diaphragm, and, lastly, feel the air traveling into your upper chest. As you exhale, breathe out completely from the low belly, diaphragm, and chest. The inhalation and exhalation are about the same length."

Three-Part or Complete Breath Strategy

- Sit comfortably in good posture; lie down if necessary.
- Take a few belly breaths to relax.
- Inhale slowly and steadily.
- Fill the belly, expand the diaphragm, and breathe fully into your lungs and chest.
- Exhale slowly and steadily.
- Breathe out from the low belly, diaphragm, and chest. Chest and ribs come back to a neutral state.
- Notice the sensations and return to abdominal breathing.
- Practice five of these breaths once or twice daily.

Anne followed my instructions, and her breathing deepened and became slightly more rhythmic. Still, she coughed and squirmed a bit in her seat as she practiced. At our next session, I decided to show her "constructive rest," an antigravity position that helps put abdominal breathing into action in the most natural way possible, by lying in a supine position. I knew that Anne would eventually learn abdominal breathing by having all of these methods at her disposal.

Constructive Rest

"Another good way to learn abdominal breathing is to get into the 'constructive-rest' position," I suggested. "If you're okay with this, I'd like you to lie on the floor mat." I handed her a small pillow to support her neck and a couple of larger ones to place beneath her knees.

After an awkward silence, Anne agreed to lie on the mat and I helped her place the pillows. "Now, put one hand on your lower belly, the other on your chest, and think about breathing abdominally and sending the oxygen to your belly. Remind yourself to breathe in fully and exhale fully.

Imagine that as your breath deepens, your muscles relax, your body lengthens, and your chest and abdomen expand."

Anne's breath immediately began to deepen, and I noticed a shift in her facial muscles. The lines in her forehead began to smooth and her jaw released. Her eyes softened, her delicate hands loosened their grip, and she seemed more at ease, more present. I reminded her to watch the rise and fall of her belly. "Remember to breathe out completely, because relaxation occurs on the exhalation."

Anne's eyes began to water, and I asked if she wanted to talk about what was going on. "No, but it seems like I understand how you are telling me to breathe and I'm more aware of feeling certain emotions when I breathe this way. I'm not sure this will necessarily be good for me, but I'm willing to try."

Constructive-Rest Strategy

- Lie down on your back on a firm surface.

- Keep your knees bent and feet on the floor about hip width apart.

- Support your head with a small pillow or rolled-up towel.

- Bend your arms at the elbow and rest your hands on your belly or by your sides.

- Relax your muscles, scanning from the top of your head to your toes.

- Think about "letting go" rather than engaging any of your muscles.

- Focus on abdominal breathing, which happens easily in this antigravity position.

- Observe the rise and fall of your belly as you breathe.

- Allow your body to lengthen and expand.

- Rest in this position for five to twenty minutes once or twice daily.

- Notice how you feel after each session.

Constructive rest, sometimes called "active rest," is a good position for learning the abdominal or three-part breath. However, you want to get to the point where you are able to practice these belly-breathing methods while sitting, standing, or walking. Ten to twenty minutes of practice yields mental, physical, and emotional benefits. While constructive rest is a relaxation technique unto itself, it is also beneficial as a prelude to sleep or when having difficulty remaining asleep.

As we ended the session, I gave Anne the assignment of breathing in the constructive-rest position for ten to twenty minutes, once a day. "Notice what comes to mind during these practice sessions. We don't have to talk about the thoughts or feelings that arise unless you want to. Just pay attention to whatever you experience."

Anne and I spent the next weeks working on her breathing, improving her ability to relax, and talking about her strained relationship with Justin as he continued to shun her attempts to connect. I suggested that she back off for now, as her hovering was probably exacerbating his anger and resentment.

Anne glared at me, her face flushing. "How do I stop caring for my son? How do I stop worrying about his safety and well-being? You are asking me to let go of the most important part of my life. Nothing matters to me as much as my family, and I'm worried about Justin."

I gently reminded her that Justin was in good hands with his therapist and that he needed to get help from someone other than her right now. "It is not that he doesn't love you," I reassured her. "He just has to figure out for himself what is going on, how to build friendships, and what his next steps are after high school. Some of this will involve you and Stephen, but much of it he needs to do on his own and within the framework of his peer group. He will come back to you in time. In the meantime, it would be useful for you to focus on your own needs and how to make this time in your life more gratifying."

Anne admitted that paying attention to her own needs had never been a priority. "My mother taught me that thinking too much about myself was selfish and unbecoming."

"Tell me more," I encouraged her.

In an instant, Anne shut down again, as if I'd crossed an invisible line. Her resistance to speaking about her inner world concerned me, but I decided that if we kept working on the relaxation techniques, she would begin to trust me enough to open up and share more of her story. Either way, the skills she was learning would serve her well.

The next time I met with Anne, something about her seemed different. I asked how her week had gone.

"I practiced breathing in the constructive-rest position at least once a day, sometimes twice," she said. "At first, it took effort just to get myself into position. After a few days, I began looking forward to my time to lie down, relax, and just focus on breathing. I've definitely begun to enjoy the constructive rest." She smiled warmly and told me that long ago she used to enjoy practicing yoga.

I asked Anne if she wanted to talk about anything in particular. "Yes," she said. "Justin began his support group and likes the other kids so far. Stephen and I bought him a cell phone, and he seems to be connecting with more of his peers. For the first time in almost two years, he's been talking to me. I'm so relieved."

"That's great," I replied. "Anything else?"

"Well, as you know, I've been smoking most of my life to relax and unwind. Now that I've been practicing the breathing, even when I go outside to smoke, the stench seems to permeate the house. The breathing is giving me something positive to focus on when I need to relax, rather than instantly reaching for a cigarette. I've been cutting back. A number of times, I chose not to smoke and instead got myself into the constructive-rest position. It definitely helps. Other times, when I'm on autopilot, I go for the smoke. Sometimes I want to go numb, and smoking does that for me. I need to rethink the way I care for myself. Clearly, I haven't been very good at it. This is such difficult work for me, but I'm committed to doing whatever it takes to feel healthier and better about myself."

Anne adjusted her posture as she sat on the couch; she still looked fragile and tired, but more approachable. Her breathing seemed more fluid and regular. I complimented Anne on her achievements of cutting back on smoking and making some important self-observations. Then, uncharacteristically, I decided to reveal something from my own experience with cigarette addiction, hoping my self-disclosure would pave the way for Anne to do more of the same: "I struggled with my own cigarette habit, and the abdominal breathing helped me conquer the addiction. Whenever I craved a cigarette, I would go outside, regardless of the weather, and practice deep-breathing exercises. The more the breathing became ingrained in me, the less I wanted to smoke, until I finally quit. You will know when it's time for you to give up the smoking. In the meantime, just keep practicing the breathing in any or all of the ways that we discussed."

The Relaxation Response

At our next session, I asked Anne if she was interested in learning another technique known as the "relaxation response." She readily agreed.

Relaxation response is a term that was coined by Herbert Benson in the mid-1970s. Benson popularized the ancient technique of meditation through research and scientific validation. He found that the relaxation response was the counterpoint to the "fight-or-flight" response. Relaxation occurs when the body no longer perceives danger and the functioning of the autonomic nervous system returns to normal. The body releases chemicals and the brain sends signals that make the muscles and organs slow down. Metabolism decreases, as do heart rate, blood pressure, and muscular tension. Breathing becomes slower and deeper, leading to diminished anxiety, irritability, and pain levels. There is also an increase in blood flow to the brain, creating a calming effect, and an increase in energy, motivation, and concentration. Initiation of the relaxation response also helps with sleep disorders.

I told her we would take about ten minutes to practice this method, which was a slight variation of Benson's original technique. We began by focusing on the breath, the lowest common denominator for any relaxation training. I suggested, "Straighten yourself up in a comfortable sitting position. You will automatically breathe more deeply and efficiently when you are in good postural alignment. Uncross your arms and legs. Relax your shoulders so they fall naturally over your torso. Gently press your lower back against the couch or use one of the pillows for support. Lift up your chest bone and let your lower back continue to sink down into the back of the couch. Don't worry about your posture after you begin this exercise, just allow yourself to relax into it."

I encouraged Anne to remove her glasses and to loosen the top button of her pants so she could breathe more fully. "Relax your closed eyes." I noticed her eyes fluttering, as though she was having difficulty with this instruction. "You don't have to do anything that makes you feel uncomfortable," I told her. "These are only suggestions."

"I'm ready to do this. My body is just being rebellious. I'm still not used to relaxing. It all feels strange, but I want to learn."

"You will. Relax your eyes closed, allowing your eyes to roll slightly upward without straining them. Relax all of your facial muscles, especially the little muscles around your eyes and jaw. Part your lips and relax your tongue. Let your face become serene and expressionless. Allow your whole body to relax into the couch, feeling fully supported. Feel the contact that your feet are making with the floor and feel your feet being fully supported. Remain still and notice the rise and fall of each breath without manipulating the breath in any way. Just observe the sensation of the breath in your body. Now repeat the word *in* to yourself as you breathe in, and *out* as you breathe out. Notice the rise and fall of each breath. When your mind wanders, gently bring your attention back to your breath. Thoughts are like the clouds passing by in the sky. Let them keep moving through. Allow any sound or distractions to serve as cues to bring you back to the breath. Most importantly, just allow yourself to be in the present moment without judgment."

Anne and I practiced this exercise silently together. I reminded her a few times to *breathe in* and *breathe out* and to gently and lovingly bring her attention back to the breath whenever her mind wandered. After about ten minutes of practice, I told her, "Release the repetition of the words *in* and *out* and slowly bring yourself back into the room, back into the present moment, and, when you are ready, gradually begin opening your eyes." Once she opened her eyes and had a moment to adjust, I asked her what she had noticed. Anne said, "I don't think I was doing it right. I couldn't concentrate or remain still, and the barrage of thoughts never stopped, although I do feel quite relaxed."

I assured Anne, "Taking the time to sit still and focus on the breath at any given time is a form of relaxation. It is also considered to be a form of meditation." Additionally, this technique and the breath work are vehicles for developing mindfulness. It takes time and practice for people to feel like they are mastering this skill. The most common challenges involve quieting the mind and keeping out intrusive thoughts. The best thing to do is to stop resisting thoughts. Allow the thoughts to pass without dwelling on them. Thoughts are a natural activity. Meditation can be a way to experience greater inner peace. This peace comes about not by eliminating thoughts, but by tuning in to the silence, the gap that is naturally present between our thoughts. Sometimes we find our way into the gap and experience the sensation of suspended time and space. This is perhaps the exception for most of us. Nevertheless, every time we sit and practice meditation, we derive a multitude of physical and psychological benefits, even when it feels like nothing is happening.

Relaxation and Meditation Technique

- Sit comfortably with the lower back supported. If necessary, lie down.

- Take a few deep breaths to relax the mind and body.

- Close the eyes and relax all facial muscles.

- Repeat the word *in* as you breathe in, and *out* as you breathe out.

- Notice the rise and fall of each breath.

- When your mind wanders, gently bring your attention back to the breath.

- Allow your thoughts to keep moving through like clouds passing by.

- Let sounds and distractions serve as cues for bringing your focus back to the breath.

- Accept whatever thoughts or feelings come to mind.

- Open your eyes gradually after the allotted time.

- Notice how you feel after the practice session.

- Practice for five to twenty minutes once or twice daily.

When we stop struggling with what is naturally occurring, we can experience calm and tranquility. The idea is to have a passive attitude about thoughts without fueling them, and to continue bringing your attention back to your breath when possible. Relaxation and meditation can look and feel as though you are doing nothing, but they are powerful tools for health and healing of the mind and the body.

"Authentic relaxation is a skill you develop over time," I told Anne. "Every time you relax deeply or meditate, it is a different experience. There is always something to be gained whenever you sit and practice. There is no such thing as doing this perfectly. With each meditation, you are training yourself to settle down, pay attention, and see things as they really are. Be patient and compassionate with yourself as you learn these methods. It may not be apparent to you now, but there is a subtle yet profound transformation taking place within you every time you practice."

Anne thought for a moment and then said with determination, "I'm making a commitment to practice meditation for at least ten minutes a day. Maybe this will help me to slow down and feel more at peace with myself." "It will," I assured her. "Incorporating a relaxation practice into your life will have a major effect on your well-being. You are going to witness benefits that might be hard to imagine right now. Give it time and observe what happens."

During times of extreme emotion or crisis, abdominal breathing and relaxation may not be the first things we turn to. However, with most day-to-day challenges these practices can provide mighty inner resources. Authentic relaxation quiets the mind in such a way that allows you to better understand yourself and develop your inner potential. In 1961, Carl Jung said, "Your vision will become clear only when you look into your own heart. . . . Who looks outside, dreams; who looks inside, awakes."[4]

The following week, Anne announced, "I've been practicing the breathing every chance I get. It's been great. Every morning before getting out of bed I meditate for ten minutes, and then again after work before I prepare dinner. It feels a little weird, and sometimes I resist the feeling because letting go and relaxing can feel a bit out of control to me. That said, I can't recall ever feeling this calm. It's as if something good is washing over me. Can we practice meditation together again? I want to make sure I'm doing it right, and it feels different when you're guiding me than when I practice on my own."

"Sounds like you're doing well," I said. "Just for the record, when you meditate with someone else it is quite different from doing it alone. Listening to guided-meditation CDs or MP3s is also a different experience than practicing on your own. Guided relaxation or meditation sessions can be quite effective, but ultimately I believe it is important to be able to practice on your own. That way, wherever you go or whatever you do, you will not need anyone or any props to help to achieve a deep state of relaxation. Initially, this guidance helps to integrate new ideas and techniques, but in time you will know what cues work best for you, and your own voice will guide you into that profound place. For now, let's practice together."

Affirmations to Conquer Addiction

Anne got into a comfortable sitting position, closed her eyes, and followed my instructions. Her breathing slowed and her body relaxed. We practiced for a few minutes. Then I said, "I would like to

---

[4]   C. G. Jung, *Letters, Vol. 1: 1906–1950* (Princeton, NJ: Princeton University Press, 1973).

add something during our meditation together. This time when we practice, let's incorporate an affirmation—a simple, positive statement about some aspect of your life that you want to work on. Let's begin the meditation as usual by getting into a relaxed sitting position, in good postural alignment, and repeat the words *in* and *out* as you follow the rise and fall of each breath. Then I will add an affirmation. Just go with it and we can discuss your experience afterward."

Several minutes into the meditation, I told Anne to release the repetition of the words *in* and *out* and replace them with the affirmation *Already healed. Already whole.* "Imagine yourself, using all of your senses, already healed and already whole." Several minutes later, I suggested, "When you are ready, release the affirmation and take a few moments to relax. Then, without making fast or abrupt movements, gradually open your eyes." While Anne was in this meditative state, I wanted her to use this affirmation, because when in a relaxed mode, the mind is most receptive to suggestion. I thought the affirmation would help Anne envision a stronger, more confident self.

She slowly opened her eyes. "I think I'm getting better at this, and I like the visual image of the affirmation." Her tone changed as she said solemnly, "For thirty-three years, I've smoked. I always said I would rather smoke than eat. For five days now, I haven't touched a cigarette. I've had some edgy moments, but for the most part I'm calm and feel so good about this accomplishment. My only fear is that it won't last."

"That's a great accomplishment, Anne. You need to keep taking it one day at a time. The fact that you've gone five days without a cigarette speaks to your ability and readiness to give up smoking and embrace healthier alternatives. The breathing and meditation will continue to serve you. Every time you crave a cigarette, know that you have alternatives that will not only help you to make better choices but also enhance the quality of your life. Remember, deep breathing is the fastest way to stifle your desire to smoke."

Affirmation Strategy

- Create a list of qualities about yourself that you deem negative.

- Write an affirmation from a positive perspective countering each negative.

- Create an affirmation or positive self-statement that is simple, supportive, and attainable.

- Repeat your affirmation often.

- Practice while relaxed because that is when the mind is most receptive to suggestion.

- Anchor the affirmation in your body by pairing it with abdominal breathing.

- When you experience benefits from your current affirmations, compose and begin to practice new affirmations to counter other negative beliefs.

Affirmations practiced while in a relaxed state counteract negative thoughts and boost self-esteem. You can continue to shape your self-perception by progressively challenging negative self-beliefs and overriding them with the use of affirmations.

Anne began weaving her practice of abdominal breathing, meditation, and affirmations into her daily routine. At last, she had concrete tools to prevent or minimize her anxiety and support her as she confronted her smoking addiction. Armed with these strategies, Anne felt empowered to take greater responsibility for her health rather than relying on sheer willpower. Instead of feeling like a weak or bad person when she slipped, she would remind herself to get back to the practices that helped her feel strong and competent.

Over the next few months, things began to change for Anne. She had backed off from Justin, found herself more relaxed and energized, and started to have inklings of wanting more out of life. As her emotions became more positive and her self-confidence improved, she became aware of her lack of friendships. She no longer wanted to isolate herself, but instead wished to cultivate a greater sense of belonging. The problem for Anne was figuring out how and where to begin her efforts to connect with others. I suggested that a good start would be for her to open up to me in the safety and privacy of the therapy room.

Sharing Her Story

Over the next weeks, Anne began talking more freely with me and with Stephen. I noticed that her face became brighter and her body less rigid. She said, "I've noticed I'm more aware of how I am feeling without having to numb myself with cigarettes. I've been paying attention to the thoughts that keep coming up in my mind. Maybe it's because I'm no longer smoking, or maybe because I have options now when it comes to dealing with painful memories." Anne slowly scanned my face. She breathed in deeply and then said she wanted to talk about her past.

This was a breakthrough for her. "That's great, Anne. We'll move at whatever pace works best for you. If any topic feels too sensitive, we can stop and revisit it later."

She began: "I grew up in a middle-class town in Connecticut, the middle of five girls. Mother was strict and self-absorbed. She had rules about the way we dressed, spoke, and studied, and about whom we chose as friends. When we didn't follow orders, we paid the consequences. It wasn't uncommon for one of us to go to bed without dinner. She spanked us when we neglected our chores or disobeyed her commands. Beth and I got it the worst. On one or two occasions, Mother made me sit alone in the basement for hours. I think she forgot I was there, but I remember being terrified.

"Father was nowhere to be found when she was doling out punishments. I remember wishing he would save us from her tyranny. Father was a gentle soul who loved us when he was around, but was usually consumed with his work. He hated her mood swings. We all did. She probably should have been on medication or in therapy, but those things weren't common back then.

"I think Father disappeared during her tirades because he couldn't tolerate her fury and probably wanted to save his own neck. I never forgave him for not standing up to her or protecting us. I remember praying I could escape. I swore that once I left, I would never come back to that house of misery."

For the first time, I had some inkling of the emotional abuse that Anne and her sisters had suffered. Anne seemed relieved to be telling her story. After a reflective pause, I asked her to tell me more about her mother.

"Mother came from an abusive background herself, but it was hard to take pity on her because she was so cruel. Her mother was an alcoholic and believed in corporal punishment, and her father remained distant and absorbed in his work. Mother never spoke much about her past. Everything was about her needs, and we were all little extensions of her. Our accomplishments became about her, and she expected perfection. We were well-mannered and well-dressed, got good grades, and took all kinds of lessons before money became an issue.

"My baby sister, Kathryn, was Mother's favorite and got treated with kid gloves. Ashley, one year my junior, kept to herself and remained under Mother's radar, for the most part. She lives in North Carolina now with her family. Margaret, the eldest, helped my mother with all of us but eloped at eighteen and moved to California. Beth was nearly two years older than me. She and I were Mother's main targets. I think we reminded her of her side of the family, and for some reason she hated us for that. Except for Kathryn, we all took turns on the hot seat, but Beth won the prize for being punished the most. No one called it abuse in those days, but Mother's behavior certainly qualified."

"Tell me more about Beth," I asked.

Anne's eyes welled up. "It still hurts every time I think about Beth. She was a good sister and we were close. We were partners in crime, even though we seldom dared to deliberately do anything wrong. Beth covered for me when she could. Unwisely, she bucked Mother's authority. Beth pretended to be tough, like she wasn't affected by Mother's cruelty, but it was an act. Mother got to her in a big way."

Retreating into the Darkness

"Beth aligned herself with Father, even though he wasn't around much. After a while, he wasn't around at all. We were all teenagers, except for Kathryn, who was only four when Father left. We all felt deserted, but Beth took it the hardest. Her world began to unravel. She shut down and retreated into the darkness."

"What do you mean, 'She retreated into the darkness'?"

"Beth was Father's favorite, and when he left, she was devastated. Beth felt deeply rejected by his abandonment, and she knew that there was no longer any illusion of safety from Mother."

Several minutes of silence passed, and I asked Anne, "Can you tell me a little more about your father?"

"I think he loved us but couldn't handle Mother's rage. He used to say, 'I just want peace, love, and harmony.' It was sweet the way he would say it, but he really felt that way. We looked like the perfect family when we went to church on Sundays. No one ever would have guessed the hell that went on at home.

"I think Father began having an affair, as he disappeared for longer and longer stretches of time. Mother's mood swings, especially after Kathryn was born, must have pushed him over the edge. I was about ten when Kathryn was born. The crazier Mother got, the more Father disappeared, until he finally bailed.

"In the end, he probably just saved himself by leaving. He wanted to stay connected to us, but he didn't want to negotiate visitation with Mother. That same year, Margaret eloped. Beth and I were in high school. Ashley was in her last year of middle school, and Kathryn was in preschool. It was the end of an era."

"That must have been so difficult for all of you. How did you feel about your father's leaving?"

"I hated him. I don't think I'll ever forgive him for leaving us alone with Mother. He would call, write letters apologizing, and repeatedly proclaim his love for us. He even told us he loved our mother. He just couldn't handle her unpredictable tantrums. I never took his calls or responded to his letters. I could not understand how he chose to put his own needs first. It still infuriates me."

Being deserted by a parent can have devastating effects on children of any age. It leaves a deep wound that needs to be healed. Talking about the abandonment and understanding its effects are vital parts of resolving the losses and the accompanying emotions such as shock, confusion, guilt, fear, rage, and grief that a child experiences. It is not uncommon for the abandoned child to become depressed and suffer low self-esteem. This kind of loss can lead to feelings of distrust, resentment, and anger that often carry into adulthood.

In subsequent sessions, Anne shared how much she had been thinking and dreaming about her family, Beth, and her father's departure.

Anne continued, "Not long after they divorced, Father remarried. Mother had to sell our beautiful home, and we moved to a small rented house, where Beth and I shared a room. Because of finances, I had to cut back on dance and piano lessons, which had always been my salvation. Mother went to work as a secretary and struggled to make ends meet. I knew that she felt enormous shame that our Father walked out on her and that our lifestyle had to change so drastically. We seldom went to church anymore or did things as a family. Mother's moods became even more precarious. Publicly, however, she always put on her red lipstick and a smile. Mother prided herself on her beauty, with good reason. No one had a clue what lurked behind that gorgeous face of hers."

Each of her sisters managed in her own way. Anne silenced her voice, hid her thoughts and feelings, and did as she was told. She made a conscious decision to remain stoic in the face of the drama. She told me, "I remember repeatedly saying to myself, 'She can't hurt me if I remain invisible.'"

Beth, on the other hand, spoke back to her mother and pretended not to care when she was punished. In reality she was quite vulnerable. Anne became terrified when Beth challenged their mother. Although Beth managed to put up a good front to appear fearless at sixteen, her façade slowly crumbled after their father left, and depression set in.

Coming Undone

As Anne described her past she said, "I think we were all depressed, but Beth was the most depressed. All she wanted to do was find Father and live with him. When she realized that would never happen, she began to shut down. She used to cry herself to sleep. Sometimes I would crawl into bed with her, just to hold her. She was so sad, and Mother remained oblivious and kept doing a number on her. Sometimes Beth would say that she had nothing to live for. I thought I knew what she meant, but I never realized she was capable of hurting herself.

"Junior year, Beth's academic performance began to decline, and Mother was all over her for that, as if that would help her perform better in school. Then, first semester of senior year, she failed two courses and was told she wouldn't be able to graduate on time. Beth freaked and didn't know what to do. She told me she couldn't handle Mother finding out or staying home another year. She became desperate. I told her that she could endure whatever punishments Mother meted out and that I would help her. Beth shut down completely, even with me."

Anne's face flushed and tears began to flow. After a few moments, she composed herself, and I reminded her to breathe and waited for her to continue.

"Several days later, I came home from school and went into the basement, where I sometimes studied to get away from the madness, and there was Beth, her beautiful body dangling from a rafter." Anne shuddered but kept going. "I screamed and somehow got her down, praying she was still alive. Then I ran to dial 911. The ambulance came within minutes, although it seemed like an eternity. I held Beth until the medics took her from my arms. Mother arrived home as they were taking her out and collapsed, wailing over and over, 'My baby is dead.' I didn't know what to do, so I just stayed with Mother and tried to calm her down as they drove off with Beth."

Anne and I sat together quietly for a few moments. "Anne, I'm so sorry that you suffered this terrible loss and were so alone in it, comforting your mother instead of being comforted by her."

"The worst part for me has always been the guilt. I feel like Beth's suicide was my fault." Anne's bloodshot eyes continued to weep.

"How could you have thought that?" I asked with genuine concern.

"Beth told me that she wished she was dead, and she was so sad and desperate after Father left. I could tell she was coming undone. I should have told my mother or someone, anyone, who might have helped. I didn't do anything. Not a day goes by when I don't feel guilty." Anne sobbed as she rocked back and forth.

I tried to console Anne and help her to reframe this traumatic memory. I said, "You were a good sister to Beth. She loved you and trusted you. The dysfunction in your family affected everyone individually and collectively. How could you have possibly known that Beth's wish to be dead was for real? It's not unusual for unhappy people to say that they wish they were dead without really meaning it. I'm sure such thoughts crossed your mind, too. Even though you knew and loved Beth as you did, you could not have known that she was capable of killing herself. Beth needed help from the adults in her life, but how could you have convinced your mother of that? Your mother's instability made it impossible for you to speak with her."

For Anne, this was a watershed moment. She wept until the end of our session. I let her stay until she felt ready to drive home. At our next session, she told me that she had cried on and off throughout the week. She reported feeling sad but relieved.

For almost thirty years, Anne had hidden her feelings of loss and guilt. Sometimes we remain stuck in grief because the pain of loss keeps our loved ones alive in our minds. Or we believe that if we feel happy, it will diminish the significance of the relationship we once had. The truth is that when people we love die, our relationships with them do not die, in the sense that we continue to have feelings about them, memories of them, and thoughts about what might have been.

Because of Anne's family dysfunction, she never had the opportunity to mourn the loss of her beloved sister. Her unresolved sorrow had turned into a complicated grief, where her painful emotions were so long-lasting and severe that they interfered with her own well-being.

"Perhaps you need to find a way to forgive yourself and your parents and say good-bye to Beth. It isn't that you can ever completely resolve such a traumatic loss, but you are still living in the shadow of Beth's death and it is causing you pain."

We talked over the next few months about Beth and their relationship, and Anne continued to practice breathing, meditation, and self-affirmation strategies. Soon thereafter, she came to her session with another breakthrough: "I realize now that all these years I have felt such guilt over Beth's suicide and that I was the one who survived the wrath and craziness of my mother. How I wish Beth could have done the same. Although my life is far from perfect, I've gone on to have so many wonderful experiences. I married a good, loving man and have been blessed with two beautiful children. If only Beth could have endured the suffering a little longer, she too could have escaped and created a decent life for herself." Anne sat silently.

Learning to Forgive

Weeks later, Anne announced, "Beth will always be close to my heart, but I'm beginning to accept that it really wasn't my fault. You were right. We were all in the same boat. In fact, each of us used to say we couldn't wait to get away and that death would probably be a better alternative to living with Mother. Beth did get eerily depressed those last few days, but I never imagined that meant she could possibly kill herself. It still breaks my heart, but I'm getting better at missing her without having to punish myself and shut others out. But I do find myself still feeling infuriated with my parents. They should have known better, they were the adults."

Over the next few sessions we centered on Anne forgiving her parents as well as herself. I suggested that she examine her story and find a way to reframe it. "Instead of focusing on the old story riddled with pain and suffering, think about creating a new narrative, a new way of interpreting your past," I suggested. "Perhaps you can focus on the life that you have created for yourself. For instance, you had the power to leave your family of origin and start your own family. You did not repeat your history or remain a victim. You survived a difficult childhood, created your own beautiful family, and stopped the cycle of abuse for your children. These are huge accomplishments and have taken immense courage. Now you are in the process of transforming yourself further as you tap into your strengths. Your healing is well under way."

Anne was ready to hear more about how forgiveness could help her transform anger and hurt into healing and peace. Author Anne

Lamott suggested that "forgiveness is giving up all hope of having had a different past."[5] Besides the reward of letting go of a painful past, there are powerful health benefits that go hand in hand with the practice of forgiveness, such as lower heart rate and blood pressure, reduced fatigue, and better sleep quality. Psychologically, forgiveness has been shown to diminish the experience of stress and inner conflict while simultaneously restoring positive thoughts, feelings, and behaviors.

The problem for many of us is that although we can choose to forgive another, in our heart of hearts, the anger or resentment lingers. So, how do we give up a grudge and forgive someone who has hurt, disappointed, or betrayed us? Fred Luskin, PhD, in his book *Forgive for Good*,[6] explains that forgiveness begins with reframing our grievance story. That's the story you tell yourself, and possibly others, about the way you were maltreated or became victimized—over and over. Dr. Luskin's book teaches how to reframe that story in such a way that you become a survivor of difficult times, or even the hero of your own story.

The following strategy for learning forgiveness draws from the work of Luskin and other researchers, along with my own work and experience as a psychologist.

---

[5] Anne Lamott, *Traveling Mercies: Some Thoughts on Faith* (New York: Anchor Books, 2000).

[6] Frederic Luskin, *Forgive for Good: A Proven Prescription for Health and Happiness* (San Francisco: HarperOne, 2003).

Forgiveness Strategy

- Take a few abdominal breaths to relax. Inquire about the root of your anger or grudge. Look at the situation fairly. Do not embellish or rearrange the details. Pay attention to how anger is holding you back and keeping you hostage.

- Review your grievance story. Now restate it and visualize yourself empowered.

- Perhaps you broke ties from a friend or family member who hurt you. Maybe you left a toxic partner. Restate your story in such a way that you become the survivor and hero in your own narrative. Look at the strengths you developed as a result of this situation. Being hurt or compromised can be a catalyst for change that leads to a new path and greater personal power.

- Bring some empathy and compassion into the mix. Blaming yourself for not seeing the signs sooner inhibits the healing process. Know that bullies and abusers have often been abused themselves. Without accepting hostile or negative behaviors, try to comprehend the suffering they endured. You can understand and forgive, without necessarily tolerating bad behavior.

- Create a ritual that says goodbye to the past as you once experienced it. Welcome the love and support that you now invite into your life. For example, light a candle and say a prayer or affirmation to symbolize the brightness of the moment and the days ahead; or gather some friends to celebrate the end of an era and the beginning of a new phase of life.

- Continue to build supportive relationships. Getting support will strengthen your ability to forgive and let go of the old narrative. Notice how feelings of anger and sadness diminish as self-esteem grows.

Anne embraced this forgiveness strategy. It deepened her insights about Beth and her past. She began to acknowledge her strengths and that she was indeed the hero of a painful past. Her beautiful family was the greatest testimonial to her success. The wounds she incurred as a child remained, at least in part. Changing her thoughts and behaviors as an adult was going to take time. Anne had been burned so many times by the important people in her early life that isolating herself became her way of remaining safe from further harm. Now she began to realize that this behavior was no longer serving her needs. Anne had to find ways to connect with others outside her immediate family. Her work was becoming clear, but still there were missing pieces.

"What happened after you left for college?" I asked.

"Just as I'd promised myself, I never returned home, except for an occasional visit. I seldom spoke to my sisters, Father, or Mother once I left. Margaret and Ashley both moved out of state, but they managed to maintain a relationship with each other and occasionally had contact with our parents. Kathryn lived nearby, and she spoke frequently to our mother and father, something I still resent. I chose to keep my distance from everyone because I wanted a new life unencumbered by my past.

"Stephen and I met freshman year of college, and I loved how much fun he was. I knew he would be a good balance for me and would help me not take everything so seriously. We lived together off campus junior year and got married shortly after graduation. We only invited our two best friends to our justice-of-the-peace wedding. It was a beautiful autumn day, and I felt so lucky to have found this wonderful man.

"Two years later, my beautiful Matthew was born. We fell madly in love with our boy, and on his first birthday we decided to start trying for another baby. I got pregnant with Justin faster than anticipated. We were elated. We didn't have many friends, but we had each other and that was all I ever wanted.

"One day, about three years before I came to see you, I got a call from Kathryn that Mother was sick. She'd been diagnosed with pancreatic cancer. Kathryn asked for my help, and although I hadn't seen either of them in several years, I felt obligated. Mother had gotten so frail and gaunt. My old fear of her had turned into pity. I visited her often and treated her kindly as she slowly wasted away. We never spoke about the past, and I felt so sad when she died, longing for the mother I never had.

"We all came together for the memorial service. Even my father showed up, although I couldn't bring myself to speak with him. A cordial hello was all I could muster."

As Anne shared these memories, she wept, stopping several times to catch her breath. In trusting herself and trusting me, she had taken the first step toward making an authentic, intimate connection with someone other than Stephen. Sharing her story with me was an opportunity for her to practice opening up with someone who would listen and accept her without judgment. I knew this would empower Anne to risk opening up with other people in her life.

Over time, Anne reached out to Kathryn and they began meeting on occasion. Anne had already connected with Margaret and Ashley—after their mother's passing—and was now thinking about visiting them after Justin left for college. She was reclaiming her family, another important step for her healing.

Putting the Pieces Together

Over the next few months, Anne also became more open with Stephen about aspects of her past and their marriage. It had been close to twenty years since they'd had any real time alone together, and she wanted to make plans as a couple. She also wished to develop a more fulfilling social life now that their nest would soon be empty, with Justin readying for college.

Our conversations and Anne's mindfulness practices facilitated new insights that allowed her to liberate herself from destructive behavior patterns. Anne succeeded in giving up her cigarette addiction. Having learned to trust me, she felt ready to open up to family, a few potential friends, and certain colleagues. After about a year of our meeting together regularly, she cultivated friendships with a few women she had met through her renewed yoga practice. It was as if Anne had emerged from her cocoon and rejoined the world of the living.

And the initial reason she'd come to see me: Justin. Once away at college, he did well academically, developed a group of good friends, and began playing in a band. When he came home on break, he let Anne into his world, albeit tentatively. Gradually, their relationship evolved into a more loving and respectful one.

Like Anne, we each have our own unique life journey. We move from event to event, at times feeling the joy in our life and at other times the pain. Connecting with others helps to alleviate suffering, and sharing our story helps us learn about ourselves while bonding with others. Self-disclosure with those we can trust teaches us that, although our personal journey is distinct, we all share the same human condition and frequently have similar experiences in common.

Anne's self-esteem slowly transformed. She became better able to feel and tolerate her inner life as she opened up and incorporated the mindfulness strategies. She continued to share her story one layer at a time, honoring her boundaries, making sure she felt safe along the way. In time, Anne trusted me to help her explore and navigate through other old wounds and current obstacles. We became partners in moving her beyond a painful past and into the moment, able to embrace the richness of her life.

Research shows that talking therapies work just as well whether you are young or old, male or female, gay or straight, working-class or middle-class, educated or not. Everyone benefits from being authentic, sharing with others, and feeling heard and understood. Arming ourselves with simple mindfulness practices, such as abdominal breathing, meditation, forgiveness, and connecting with trusted others, contributes to our health and happiness, the ability to find inner peace, and the realization of goals and dreams. And what in life is more important than that?

CHAPTER THREE
Looking for Love

Carolyn

Entering my office for her first session, Carolyn was dressed impeccably in a dark-gray suit, a pale-blue silk blouse that reflected the color of her wide-set eyes, and chic patent leather pumps. She greeted me with a friendly, firm handshake. Tall, attractive, and lithe, Carolyn, a thirty-two-year-old attorney living alone, repeatedly got involved in unfulfilling relationships with unavailable men. She also had trouble making friends with women. She immediately dropped her professional demeanor to speak candidly about her disappointing past relationships with men. As I listened to her history, I began to understand the source of her problems in relating to others and her inability to build more satisfying relationships.

Loneliness and Isolation

Carolyn struggled with feelings of loneliness and isolation—the primary reason that most women and men decide to seek out therapy. Although social media and technology help us to connect more readily, in recent years the depth of our connections with others seems to have been compromised. According to the 2010 US Census, a whopping thirty-two million people lived alone in the United States. The percentage of people living alone has grown significantly over the past forty years, from 17 percent of total households in 1970 to 27 percent in 2010. A widely cited 2006 study from the *American Sociological Review* found that Americans have one-third fewer close friends and confidants than they had just two decades ago. Sadly, one in four individuals said they had no close confidants at all.[7]

Loneliness is a complex human emotion that can make you sick, amplify your experience of pain and depression, weaken your immune system, interfere with your ability to sleep, and shorten your life span. Most people experience feelings of loneliness, detachment, and isolation at one time or another, often during times of transition such as moving to a new location, when children leave home, during a breakup or divorce, and after the death of a loved one. However, when loneliness endures over long stretches of time, as it clearly had for Carolyn, the implications can be serious. The chronically lonely crave human contact, but their state of mind can make it difficult for them to form healthy connections with others.

In *Loneliness,* John Cacioppo, one of the nation's leading scholars on loneliness, reported that MRI brain scans of chronically lonely people look different from those of their more socially connected counterparts. Lonely people are more likely to be stressed, which not only increases wear and tear on the body by keeping it in alert mode, but also interferes with the ability to relax and to recharge.[8]

Cacioppo's findings suggest that the brains of the lonely are wired to view the world through a negative lens. Loneliness, he reports, increases the risk of death about as much as smoking cigarettes and more than obesity or lack of exercise. Cacioppo found that one out of five people indicate having the subjective experience of long-standing loneliness. These are people willing to report their experience of isolation; the problem is likely more widespread.

The quality of our relationships is arguably the most important factor in our ability to feel fulfilled, deeply connected to our world, and

---

[7] Jeffrey Boase, John B. Horrigan, Barry Wellman, and Lee Rainie, "The Strength of Internet Ties: The Internet and Email Aid Users in Maintaining Their Social Networks and Provide Pathways to Help when People Face Big Decisions," *Pew Internet and American Life Project* (January 25, 2006).

[8] John T. Cacioppo and William Patrick, *Loneliness: Human Nature and the Need for Social Connection* (New York: W. W. Norton & Company, 2009).

authentically happy. Also, our sense of self comes from the connections we are able to form with others. Not knowing how to develop and sustain healthy relationships can wreak havoc on the mind, body, and spirit.

Women, especially, suffer when they are unable to make friendships. They often falsely believe that finding a romantic partner, even an unsuitable or unavailable one, will alleviate their loneliness. The truth is that about half of all marriages fail, and many of the ones that do not fail are compromised. It therefore behooves women to develop an effective support network beyond that of a romantic relationship. Based upon the available research and my clinical experience, the happiest women have embraced this truth.

Thankfully, building friendships and a strong support system are within reach for women willing to practice certain strategies and skills designed to help them better connect with others. This is what I began exploring with Carolyn as I asked her to tell me about her family history.

Sorting Out the Past

Carolyn's mother was a homemaker and her father was a professor at a nearby college in the heart of New Hampshire. Her middle-class family valued education, art, and culture, and were members of the local Methodist church. Carolyn was the middle child, with her older brother, Jeffrey, two years her senior, and her sister, Ellen, two years her junior. Jeffrey married his high school sweetheart and moved several states away for work. He had two young sons and visited only for Christmas and other occasional events. Ellen, a kindergarten teacher, had recently married a man she had met skiing. They lived near her parents.

Carolyn, attractive, engaging, and always a standout student, came to Boston for college and stayed to attend a prestigious law school. Sadly, she repeatedly found herself drawn to unavailable men. Each successive failed relationship left Carolyn feeling more perplexed and alone. She came to see me to understand her underlying issues and receive guidance in making behavioral changes and better choices.

I asked her to tell me more about her specific memories of growing up, whatever came to mind. "I essentially raised myself and my siblings," she said. "When I was six, my grandmother had an operation that left her partially disabled. My mom spent almost every day caring for her, eventually placing her in a nursing home, but still visiting her daily. When my mother was home with us, she was exhausted or preoccupied. I liked cooking, so I started doing most of the meal preparation for our family in fourth grade. My dad worked all day, and came home to eat the dinner I'd made. He'd help with the cleanup, say a few words to us, and then retreat to his downstairs study. We weren't supposed to disturb him when he was working. Jeffrey was always off with friends and Ellen counted on me for everything, and I didn't want to let her down.

"It was like I was a little adult, managing the household. I don't remember ever just being a kid. A few times I tried inviting classmates over, but they couldn't come because their parents didn't like that neither of my parents was around.

"I was always in charge, and I kind of liked it. I took my job seriously—at home and at school. I had no idea this wasn't how everyone lived. Kids made fun of me for being serious and bossy, so I eventually stopped trying to make friends. The girls never included me in parties or sleepovers. I felt like such a misfit, except in my caretaker role at home and getting straight A's at school. Even now, I find it a struggle to let go of leadership roles and connect with my peers as an equal."

Carolyn had just given me a glimpse into her past and the intense feeling of loneliness she experienced at home and at school. She gazed out the window as she continued to share her story, checking her emotions to maintain her composure.

She continued, "My grandmother died just after I turned twelve and Mom fell into a deep depression for about two years. She cried all the time. I thought it was odd that she was more attached to her mother than she was to her own children. I'm not sure about my siblings, but I began to feel irrelevant. Then, around fifth or sixth grade, I started feeling nervous much of the time. I just hoped that nothing bad would happen to our family. I couldn't take on any more."

As I let a moment of silence pass, I looked into Carolyn's eyes and said, "Something really bad had already happened. There was a role reversal, and instead of your parents taking care of you, you took care of them, your siblings, the chores, and all at such an early age. Living like that must have been so difficult for you."

Carolyn looked stoic, but finally let a few tears roll down her cheeks. She said, "Honestly, it was all I knew. Only years later did I realize just how abnormal it was."

Carolyn was a "parentified child." *Parentification* happens when there is a role reversal between parent and child. Carolyn relinquished her own needs and accommodated the implicit demands of her parents to secure the nurturance, attention, and guidance she so deeply desired. This complicated her emotional development and her ability to relate to other children her age. As an adult, she continued to struggle to form healthy relationships with both men and women.

According to developmental psychology, healthy social and emotional development requires that children have a caring, nurturing relationship with at least one parent or primary caregiver. Carolyn did not experience healthy, age-appropriate attachments with either of her parents, her siblings, or her schoolmates. In families where a parent must spend time caring for an aging or severely disabled parent, or where there is mental illness, addiction, or another significant and ongoing distraction or imbalance, the children often grow up feeling anxious, lonely, and, on some level, abandoned. Children raised in such families often suffer from low self-esteem, anxiety, depression, learning difficulties, and an impaired ability to form healthy relationships with peers. If the issues go unaddressed, they can continue into adulthood, possibly for life.

I frequently get asked, "Can people who have had a painful or traumatic childhood go on to lead happy and fulfilling lives?" Although Sigmund Freud believed that a child's basic personality was formed by age five, which suggests that people with a childhood characterized by neglect or abuse might never overcome these early obstacles, recent research has debunked this theory. Today, mental health professionals across virtually all theoretical and practice approaches endorse the perspective that, with psychological intervention, good support networks, and specific learned strategies, people can develop the resilience to overcome much of the damage caused by an injurious childhood. Over the years, I have seen many individuals overcome unimaginable trauma and lead healthy and gratifying lives. It is possible to rewrite your script and move from the role of victim to the role of hero.

Connecting Within Through Journal Writing

The first major step in overcoming a painful past involves sharing your story with the associated feelings and developing insight into the trauma or hurt that occurred early on in life. Examining your past and connecting the dots between then and now enables you to make better choices going forward. Journal writing is a powerful tool that can inform and instruct you on the path to greater insight and self-knowledge.

James Pennebaker's pioneering work in *Writing to Heal*[9] and subsequent research on the topic of journal writing confirm what many of us have intuitively known: *journal writing is a highly effective way to manage stress and to identify and cope with a wide range of problematic behaviors.* Journaling is strongly encouraged in the field of psychology and medicine; it fosters insight, self-awareness, and behavioral change. Behavioral psychologists often say, "If you can track it, you can change it."

Journaling includes recording personal impressions, daily experiences, and evolving insights as well as reflections about oneself and one's relationships, dreams, fantasies, and creative musings. Journaling allows the writer another avenue to process thoughts, impressions, and feelings. Looking back at earlier entries can foster the writer's ability to gain knowledge from past events and circumstances that might otherwise go unnoticed. A repetitive, self-destructive behavior becomes more apparent when observed through multiple journal entries over time.

Journal writing supports the writer, never judges, and helps to clarify and refine complicated thoughts and emotions. Regular journal writing is another vehicle for developing mindfulness. Like meditation, journal writing helps to clear the mind by transcribing emotional clutter onto the

[9] James W. Pennebaker, *Writing to Heal: A Guided Journal for Recovering from Trauma & Emotional Upheaval* (Wheat Ridge, CO: Center for Journal Therapy, 2004).

written page. Once the mind is clear, the writer is better able to observe her or his behaviors and make way for fresh thoughts and perspectives. Journaling provides a forum that can be both cathartic and revelatory.

I encouraged Carolyn to write in a journal once or twice a day for at least ten minutes. It would complement our work together and serve as an added support for Carolyn, helping her to observe and better understand certain repetitive and self-defeating behaviors that contributed to her feelings of loneliness and isolation. Raising Carolyn's consciousness about her behavioral patterns in her relationships with men was the first step toward her making more positive and thoughtful choices.

Benefits of Journal Writing

- Clarifies goals and dreams.
- Refines understanding of the past.
- Fosters self-expression and self-discovery.
- Facilitates critical reflection about your behavior.
- Defines the roles of the important players in your life.
- Improves the ability to regulate strong emotions.
- Helps to process thoughts and problem-solve.
- Deepens understanding of your relationships.
- Reduces stress and improves resilience and feelings of happiness.
- Helps you move through the grieving process.
- Promotes behavioral change.
- Creates a great companion wherever you go.

You can always count on your journal to be there for you. Perhaps it seems like a poor substitute for a relationship, but you'll be surprised by the value you derive from journaling. It is a great resource for observing shifts in your inner world and outer behaviors. I suggested to Carolyn that she begin by writing about her loneliness and what gets in her way when it comes to connecting with others. She could also write about what makes her feel happy and alive.

Begin your journaling practice by buying a notebook that you can carry with you. You also might want to keep a separate one by your bed to record dreams. Keeping your journal as a private file on your computer is another option. Choose any method that enables you to write consistently for at least ten minutes a day. Some people find that lingering over the writing takes them into a state of reflection about the past, present, or future. Others prefer to track their thoughts about particular subjects, such as dreams and certain behaviors like smoking, eating, or mood variations. Writing helps you to identify and clarify goals, wishes, and your truest emotional reality without inhibition. You might even consider a brief meditation as a prelude to your journal writing. In this way, you will create the condition for even greater focus and lucidity in your thoughts and writing.

There are many ways to keep a journal. You may wish to consider the type of journal you would like to keep. There are four kinds of journaling that I am proposing here: free association, gratitude, sentence prompts, and dreams.

Free-Association Journaling

In a free-association journal the writer records whatever comes to mind. This type of journaling helps with processing events and clarifying thoughts. It is a venue for noticing feelings, insights, and matters of the heart. Free-association journaling also creates an opportunity for recording life lessons and reflecting on important questions. This kind of journal is a way of investigating the unconscious mind. In a relaxed state, record all passing thoughts without judgment or censorship.

- Sit in a comfortable position.
- Close your eyes for a moment or two.

- Take a few abdominal breaths to relax your mind and body.
- Ask yourself: "How am I feeling right now?" Notice what comes to mind.
- When you are ready, open your eyes.
- Begin writing your thoughts down without judgment or censorship.
- Do not worry about grammar or content.
- Just write.
- Write about your thoughts, feelings, ideas, observations, dreams, or fantasies.
- There are no rules except to keep writing, ideally for about ten minutes daily.

Gratitude Journaling

In a gratitude journal the writer makes daily entries about several events for which she or he is grateful. The idea behind the gratitude journal is to strengthen the part of the brain that focuses on positive thoughts and deepens the capacity for appreciation. This type of journaling is strongly associated with diminished depression and the heightened experience of inner peace and well-being. Gratitude has been shown to raise your happiness quotient, especially when journal entries are made on a regular basis.

- Sit in a comfortable position, perhaps even sit in bed.
- Close your eyes and take a few abdominal breaths, relaxing your mind and body.
- Think about *What am I grateful for?* Visualize whatever comes to mind.
- Begin writing about whatever you feel grateful for without censoring your thoughts.
- Write down whatever experiences come to mind. For example, write about feeling grateful for a good conversation with a friend, a walk with your dog, a deep meditation, a beautiful sunset, or a good meeting at work.
- Ideally, list or write about three to five such events daily.

Sentence-Prompts Journaling

In a sentence-prompts journal the writer uses open-ended questions or incomplete sentences to evoke thoughts, feelings, and associations. Sentence prompts evoke thoughts and feelings that might otherwise not come to mind. This is another way to enter your journal-writing experience.

- Get into a comfortable sitting position and take a few deep breaths.
- Choose a prompt, examples of which follow below.
- Write for ten minutes or longer, if you choose.

Examples of Sentence Prompts:

A risk I am willing to take today is _____.

My life feels most harmonious when I _____.

My goal today is _____.

My relationship will improve when _____.

I believe that _____.

I have always wanted to _____.

I have decided to _____.

My greatest strengths are _____.

I am grateful for _____.

I will always remember _____.

I love _____.

I am happiest when _____.

I feel fulfilled when _____.

What can I do about _____?

Dream Journaling

In a dream journal the writer records her or his dreams upon awakening. Dreams can be a powerful source of insight. Once you begin keeping this kind of journal, you are likely to improve your dream recall. Your dreams are a window into your subconscious mind, which is a powerful way to understand your inner world. Sometimes, in the time it takes to say "Good morning" to your partner, your dream can slip away. At first, you may only remember fragments or images from your dreams, but in time you will find that you have access to more vivid recollections.

- Keep a journal and writing implement within reach of your bed.
- Write down your dreams or key words from the dream immediately upon awakening.
- Notice the themes of your dreams.
- Think about how they relate to your everyday life.
- Use this understanding to inform your choices and behavior.

Healing Childhood Trauma Through Connection

After about six sessions, Carolyn found that journal writing took some of the sting out of her experience of loneliness. She began by keeping a combination of free-association and sentence-prompt journals. Journaling brought up some painful buried recollections. Since one of her goals was to understand the reasons behind her unsuccessful relationships with men and women, I encouraged her to continue writing about concerns and fears regarding her relationships. Together we began making connections between her current loneliness and her unresolved childhood experiences.

As we observed with Anne in Chapter Two, when getting in touch with one's early childhood memories, particularly memories from a challenging history, the old emotional pain can sometimes resurface with a vengeance. With the right support, insight gained from therapy, and use of mindfulness strategies, the pain can be managed successfully. Carolyn was struggling to overcome her long history of loneliness and isolation, and in doing so she needed to look at the origins of these feelings and figure out how to change her story moving forward.

She arrived at her next appointment late, explaining: "I haven't slept well since our last session. I could hardly get out of bed this morning. I've been trying so hard to break through my loneliness by getting out more, but I like my little apartment, where I can control my world. I know this sounds crazy, but I prefer keeping to myself. A couple of nights ago I agreed to go to a party, thinking it would be good for me, and I've been anxious ever since. I get so worked up about being in social situations. I'm fine at work. And I'm fine being alone with a guy, but parties terrify me. Maybe I'm just too sensitive to start building relationships and getting close to new people. Maybe I am just better off alone. I don't know."

I asked Carolyn what she thought her fear about meeting new people might be about. She reflected for a moment and took a few breaths before answering, "I told you how I was considered a bossy kid and didn't have many friends, right?" I nodded. "Well, I remembered an incident during one of my recent journal-writing sessions. One day when I was in first grade, a group of kids on the school bus pinned me down on my seat and wouldn't let me get off at my stop. They laughed at me as they held me back. I was so paralyzed with fear that I couldn't even scream to tell the bus driver. He never realized I'd missed my stop. When he got to the end of his route, instead of taking me home, he had me get off and walk alone."

Carolyn's eyes began to well up. "Six years old and I had to find my way home alone. When I got home, there was no one to tell. My mom was at my grandmother's, Jeff had gone home with a friend that day, and Ellen was at the babysitter's house. I just crawled into bed and sobbed. I was petrified of the bus ride home after that and sat in the front row, even though I hated the bus driver. I never told my parents. But something changed for me that day."

I agreed and added, "How awful to be so young, alone, and cast out to fend for yourself, and then to not have anyone at home to comfort you. My guess is that was the day you stopped trusting that the world was a safe and caring place."

Carolyn dissolved into tears. She turned her face and body away from me, toward the wall, attempting to gain control of her painful emotions. "None of the kids ever let me back in. They all thought I was such a freak. I was so lonely. Still today, I think about how cruel the kids were. If only I had had one good friend, I think it could have changed my whole life."

"I think you're right, Carolyn. A good friend might have carried you through those lonely times. You were burdened with adult responsibilities when you should have been allowed to be a carefree kid. Your parents were so involved with their own responsibilities and needs that they didn't focus on what was important for your development. The good news is that you have the rest of your life ahead of you to make personal changes and find adult friends who won't hurt or abandon you. I'm going to help you work on that.

Looking for Love in All the Wrong Places

I prompted her gently by saying, "For now, let's continue to uncover your history. Tell me about your relationships with men."

Carolyn continued: "Even though I felt sort of invisible growing up as a too-skinny kid with stringy brown hair, I feel attractive and much less awkward now. I usually get the guy I'm after, but inevitably things fall apart. I'm embarrassed to say this, but I've had several affairs with married men. I get into these doomed relationships and think things will be better this time around, only to realize that, again, I've gotten myself into another dead-end situation."

Carolyn shared two specific liaisons: "Several years ago, I slept with a senior partner, Robert, from the law firm where I was working at the time. That affair continued for two years. I secretly hoped he would leave his unhappy marriage and we would sail off together into the sunset. When I realized he wasn't ever planning to leave his family, and that his marriage probably wasn't as unhappy as he'd led me to believe, I ended it. I felt extremely guilty, and don't know why it took me so long to figure out that what I was doing was wrong and not good for me. I promised myself that I'd never again be the 'other woman,' but somehow I found myself in another relationship with a married man.

"When I joined another law practice, one of the partners began asking me to lunch. I knew no one at the new firm and had no way of knowing Ted's circumstances. He didn't wear a wedding band and seemed like a sincere, sensitive guy. He had a beautiful apartment in town and we began spending more time together. Not too long after we had started sleeping together, Ted confessed that he had a wife but had been separated for about six months. He assured me his divorce was imminent."

"How did you feel when you learned he was still married?" I asked.

"Angry and kind of desperate. Here was this lovely man that I thought was falling in love with me and instead he lied to me about being married and having two young sons. He lied by omission. Again, against my better judgment, I stayed. Ted swore that his marriage was over and that he would never keep anything from me again. I wanted to believe him, but two years later he was still living in his gorgeous apartment and he was still married. About five months ago, I ended that relationship. I feel cheated and stupid for falling for these guys' stories. Worst of all, I still miss Ted.

"Most recently, I've been involved with a guy in my building. His apartment is diagonally across from mine. He's sort of a hippie type, which is not at all what I am usually attracted to. I do, however, find him oddly attractive and I know that he is single. I can hear him coming home in the evening, which I somehow find reassuring. He helps me with stuff around my apartment and doesn't want an exclusive relationship, which works for me because he isn't someone I could ever see myself ending up with. The problem is, after we sleep together, I sometimes feel even lonelier. This is really what catapulted me into therapy. It terrifies me that I'm thirty-two, still alone, and have no idea about how to find a healthy relationship."

Carolyn was smart, successful, and attractive by all standards. Yet her instincts were off when it came to choosing men. She desperately needed to figure out how to stop sabotaging her opportunities for having a healthy, loving, and mutual relationship.

You Gotta Have Friends

In our next session, I decided to detour off the topic of intimacy with men and asked Carolyn more about her friendships with women. She had previously shared with me that she had no close friends and didn't even like or trust women. She believed they were threatened by her professional success and her ability to attract men. Her childhood scars from being rejected by her peers were evident in her wish to avoid forming friendships with women as an adult. The problem was that Carolyn's rejection of women friends heightened her experience of loneliness and isolation.

Women are hardwired to crave and seek out friendships. In *The Tending Instinct,* Shelley E. Taylor consolidated findings from decades' worth of research and anecdotal references pointing to the idea that women are by nature social beings and collaborative.[10] Being connected with a community of women is, simply put, part of our DNA. Women tend to band together for protection and support. This is true across species and throughout human cultures—where women have groomed each other, tended to each other's young, nursed each other in sickness, and generally enjoyed the seemingly aimless pleasure of being together. We now know that this sociability makes women hardy and resilient.

Studies have shown that loneliness and social isolation can be as deleterious to one's health as obesity or chronic smoking. Women with a strong network of friends tend to outlive women with fewer friendships. One study of almost 3,000 nurses with breast cancer found that women without close friends were four times more likely to die from cancer than were those with ten or more friends. How close they lived or how often they had contact with their friends was not relevant to these findings.[11] Interestingly, having a spouse did not affect survival rates.

---

[10] Shelley E. Taylor, *The Tending Instinct: How Nurturing Is Essential to Who We Are and How We Live* (New York: Times Books, 2002).

[11] Young Survival Coalition, Susan G. Komen for the Cure, Advocacy Alliance, Breast Cancer Network of Strength, and Living Beyond Breast Cancer, "Joint Statement on the Breast Cancer Education and Awareness Requires Learning Young Act (or EARLY Act) of 2009 (H.R. 1740, S. 994)."

Friendships yield unique benefits for women—different from those we get from our partners and family. A 2004 study commissioned by Dove, "The Real Truth About Beauty: A Global Report," found that 70 percent of women feel more attractive and experience higher self-esteem when connected to women friends.[12]

Friendships act as a buffer against stress in our tumultuous lives. They boost our experience of happiness and well-being. Women often share their deepest secrets with each other, laugh and cry together, and talk for hours about their lives. These conversations and emotional outpourings help us navigate our way through losses and transitions. It has been shown that social support helps to lower blood pressure, protect against cardiovascular disease and dementia, and reduce the risk of depression. Research has also shown that social support heightens our sense of belonging and purpose.

Friendships often have a more positive effect on our emotional well-being than do relationships with family members. When a romantic relationship ends, women generally can turn to their friends for closeness and support. Unfortunately, this is not usually the case for men. However, research suggests that both women and men heal faster when they can rely on a network of friends.

Healthy friendships carry us through even the most challenging times and can be our most enduring and important relationships. We can live without lovers or spouses and even without our nuclear families. However, most of us cannot live fulfilling lives without friends. Yet, sadly, friendship often remains an undervalued resource in many women's lives. Learning to overcome the barriers that interfere with the ability to form strong, positive friendships is essential to emotional and physical well-being.

Healthy social relationships are a major predictor of quality of life. When we have our "tribe," "team," "sangha," or community of women friendships, we learn and grow from each other. We empathize and

[12] Nancy Etcoff, Susie Orbach, Jennifer Scott, and Heidi D'Agostino, "The Real Truth About Beauty: A Global Report," Findings of the Global Study on Women, Beauty and Well-Being, September 2004. http://www.clubofamsterdam.com/contentarticles/52%20Beauty/dove_white_paper_final.pdf (accessed January 9, 2017).

empower each other, and we inspire each other to be more than we ever thought possible on our own. We share our sorrows and disappointments, laughter and heartfelt hugs. Too often, we cut loose our friends when under pressure from our "crazy-busy" lives. Making friendship time a priority fortifies us and makes us more courageous and resilient in all that we do.

In their quest for better health, many women look first to medical attention, alternative practices, or self-help books. They often overlook a powerful weapon that can help fight illness and depression, speed recovery from illness, slow aging, and prolong life—their friendships.

I reviewed this research with Carolyn and proposed that we delve more deeply into her fears around connecting with women. Carolyn was not happy about the idea, but agreed to have this conversation. When I asked her directly about her friendships with women, her eyes brimmed with tears. She whispered with a hint of shame, "I just think that women can be cruel, and it seems like such an effort to cultivate even one friendship. I'd rather put my energy into my work and finding a good man." However, Carolyn needed to find peace and connection with the women in her life, in addition to the injured woman within herself. This needed to happen before she could have a successful relationship with a man.

Carolyn and I continued to talk about the taunting and bullying she experienced, mostly with the girls in school when she was growing up, and the lack of availability of her mother. Her anger and sadness were not far beneath the surface. She understood that the girls and women in her life had let her down and that it was easier to avoid the heartache of being disappointed in her relationships with other women than to seek them out and try to make meaningful connections. Carolyn needed to sit with the idea of taking some risks and reaching out to her peers in the name of making a few good friends. I agreed to help her each step of the way, knowing that this would be a process.

Several sessions later, Carolyn reported that Ellen, her younger sister, had announced that she was pregnant. "I am happy for her, but her pregnancy makes me feel so afraid that life is passing me by and that I'll never find love or have a family of my own."

I told Carolyn, "I'm not surprised that Ellen's pregnancy is stirring you up. She has some of the things you so deeply desire, but it may take a while still, because you are in the middle of figuring things out about yourself and your relationships. Your time will come. Besides, when a friend or family member moves forward in some major aspect of their life, it is not unusual to compare your own life to hers or his and feel inadequate or left behind. This feeling will quiet down as you experience greater fulfillment in your own life. I suggest we continue talking about your reluctance to establish a few good women friends."

"I don't know how to do this," Carolyn said. "I'm afraid of being let down. I always feel used or hurt when I try to get close to women. I feel judged or like they are competing with me. It doesn't exactly make me want to seek out their friendship."

"I know this is hard," I offered. "You've done a great deal of self-help work over the years and this has served you well in your ability to focus and develop yourself professionally. It's time to take your mindfulness practice to the next level. I suggest you begin by honing your skills for building relationships, creating conscious connections that allow you to feel true to yourself and authentic with others." Carolyn reluctantly agreed to the homework I assigned to identify several women from her life with whom she could potentially connect for coffee, a walk, or dinner. She did not have to make an actual date, just identify potential friends.

As I did with Anne, I suggested that Carolyn add affirmations to her practice of meditation. I proposed a few possibilities and asked her to choose one that resonated best, or to create her own affirmation. After about ten minutes of meditation, Carolyn would repeat this affirmation and visualize herself in the context of creating safe and supportive friendships. Then, when possible, she would write about her experience in her journal.

Friendships Affirmations

- "I make friends with ease."

- "I am open to building new friendships."

- "I attract positive and supportive people into my life."

- "My ability to communicate draws people close to me."

- "My friends nurture me and make me laugh."

- "My friendships are meaningful and rewarding."

- "I have wonderful friends who are kind and trustworthy."

- "I create lasting and loving friendships with good people."

Soon thereafter, Carolyn reported, "I have been thinking about what you said about my past and the way that has played into the choices I make in relationships with men and with women." Her journaling had helped her see how she had settled for unsatisfying romantic relationships. As a result, she decided to stop sleeping with her neighbor and to center on building friendships with women, at least for the time being.

I suggested we continue to connect her history of being a parentified child and her feelings of isolation from other girls when she was young to some current life patterns. "It makes sense that you have pursued relationships that have let you down," I said. "It's familiar. That's what you grew up with. Unconsciously, you have recreated situations in which you feel abandoned or disappointed once again. Your deep hope has been that the outcome will be different each time, but the frustration continues because of your choices. The good news is that your life is different now. You are stronger and more capable of making better relationship decisions—with men and women. Putting your mindfulness to work means being thoughtful and present in your relationships with others. For starters, try giving potential women friends a chance by spending some time with them. Experiment with trusting them, before assuming the worst or rejecting them."

Courting New Friends

Carolyn said she was thinking about contacting a few women from college. Since it had been some time since her college years, I suggested she begin with one or two of them and plan something simple like coffee or lunch together. That way, she could see whether there was a bond that could be built upon.

I also reminded her that growing a friendship with a woman was similar to a courtship. "You need to take it slowly and let things evolve. Getting to know anyone is like a dance where one person steps forward and the other back. It's much easier to do the dance slowly, especially at the beginning. Sometimes you are the one giving the invitation or support, and other times you are on the receiving end. Letting friends continue to know that you care about them and appreciate them helps strengthen the bond. Being a good friend and surrounding yourself with good friends makes the dance gratifying. Over time, you get to know the boundaries that feel safe and comfortable for you. It's easier to address or repair minor disappointments or boundary issues as they arise when you move gradually."

Friendship is one of the most precious gifts in our lives. Some of us are fortunate to have good, loving friendships beginning in childhood. Others learn later on in life how to cultivate good friends. Throughout life, the need for female friends continues. So, if you don't have your "posse" of friends, build one!

Creating a support system is a skill that takes time and practice. Here are some pointers that might help in growing your "team" of friends.

Strategies for Building Healthy Friendships

- Make building and strengthening friendships a priority. Put plans with friends in your calendar as you would any other engagement or appointment.

- Be your authentic self and you will attract like-minded people. Join clubs, events, organizations, and classes that interest you, as these are fertile ground for discovering potential friendships.

- Lose toxic friendships that consistently bring you down. These "friendships" drain the energy needed to develop satisfying and healthy relationships.

- Listen reflectively to your friends. This is perhaps the greatest gift you can give a friend. You do not have to solve their problems, just listen wholeheartedly. Take risks by connecting with someone you want to get to know. Just like with romantic relationships, we feel attracted to those we want to draw into our life space as friends.

- Allow yourself to take a chance and connect with someone who interests you.

- Invest time in your friendships. "Crazy busy" is not a good excuse for not connecting with friends. Making friendships a priority is essential for happiness and well-being. If face-to-face contact is simply not possible, this might mean keeping in touch through social media, Skype, email, and so on. It is impossible to derive the rich dividends that come from well-nourished relationships unless you invest time in building your friendships.

- Communicate authentically with your friends. Know that conflict is part of any relationship. Conflict resolution occurs when you express yourself honestly and compassionately, and then listen intently to the other person. This might be challenging initially, but will likely deepen your bond with that person. Healthy communication sometimes means agreeing to see things differently.

- Expect your friendships to change over time. A good friendship can tolerate and absorb changes that are part of personal growth. Acceptance of the other person as she changes strengthens bonds and helps both of you to thrive.

- Expand your circle of friends. Each friend brings her own unique gifts to the relationship.

- It behooves us to broaden our circle of friends so that we may nurture the many facets of our selves. One friend might stimulate a sense of adventure, another might be an inspirational mentor, another is a great shopping partner, another is great to pour your heart out to, while another is a great workout companion, and so on.

Screening Out Toxic Friends

Building friendships is a skill that often takes time and practice. I told Carolyn, "As you build an inventory of potential friends, pay attention to the people around you as you go through your day. Different people will interest you in unique ways, and the idea is to cultivate friends who satisfy varying needs or interests. It will probably be a stretch for you at first, but it is important that you reach out, continue to take risks, and connect with others." I suggested that it would be ideal if she reached out to several potential friends, so that if one person ended up disappointing her or became unavailable, she had others to draw upon.

I also mentioned that, sometimes, a friendship changes: "For instance," I explained, "if you notice a particular friend consistently leaves you feeling worse after spending time together, it may be time to reconsider the value of that relationship. It might make sense to lessen contact, or, in extreme cases, to press the 'delete friend' button. The goal is to create and keep only those friendships that nurture, support, and enrich our lives.

"Moving slowly, while you build new friendships, makes this process feel less risky. Take time getting to know each person you meet so that you don't miss indications that this might not be a good match for you. Also, as you get to know someone, be careful not to become excessively dependent on that person. It is one thing to open up and self-disclose about your life and quite another to expect anyone to be endlessly available to you. This is another good reason why a support system works best, so that we do not become overly reliant on any one person."

Respecting the boundaries in a friendship also creates the space for that connection to grow safely. An example might be not bombarding a friend with phone calls or texts or making an abundance of plans early on in a relationship. It takes time to know what level of reciprocity exists in the friendship, and this information is a barometer for a healthy alliance.

Perhaps the most important part of developing and nurturing friendships is listening deeply without judgment. We live in a culture where many of us do not feel heard or understood. In a healthy relationship, reflective listening is the ultimate gift that tends to be returned in kind. For example, when a patient feels heard in the therapy setting, something magical often happens. That person feels valued, relevant, and cared for, sometimes in profound ways. I suggest you bestow this gift upon the important people in your life or the friendships you wish to cultivate. Notice what happens when your friend feels like you really got what she said. A final piece of advice I gave Carolyn: "Give your friend the space to be herself without being quick to judge, and respect her confidentialities. This creates a haven in which you and your friend can safely share with each other."

Building a Fuller Life

Carolyn was ready to build the friendships she had been lacking for so long. Her time was limited because of her busy career, but she now took her search for smart, supportive, and fun women seriously. Her mission was clear, and she was not one to turn down a challenge.

For the next six or seven sessions, Carolyn kept her eyes open for potential friends at the gym, at work, and at whatever gatherings she attended. In a low-key but deliberate way, she scanned her world for women she thought she might want to befriend. Specifically, she contacted three college friends who lived in different parts of the Northeast. Following a flurry of emails, Facebook connections, and phone calls, they decided to meet in New York City for a weekend of culture, shopping, and fun. At first Carolyn felt anxious, but decided to take the plunge. Once she and her college buddies got to reminiscing and sharing stories about their lives, Carolyn found herself feeling a profound sense of joy. They talked and laughed into the wee hours.

Weeks later, as she filled me in, Carolyn wondered, "How could I have been missing out like this? I don't remember my time with them in college ever being such fun. I'm not used to laughing so much. We hardly slept, but when we finally did crash, I went down grinning. We're planning to meet again in the summer, and I can hardly wait."

The trip was a wonderful leap for Carolyn. I suggested she keep building on what she started. In time, she connected with a woman in her Pilates class and a fellow attorney in her office building. She began planning dinners, after-work drinks, walks, and occasional classes into her full schedule. To her amazement, Carolyn began to cherish time with her women friends.

Carolyn and I worked together on a weekly basis for almost two years. With her support system firmly in place, she felt much better about herself and her life and she no longer took solace in unhealthy relationships with unavailable men. For the first time in years, she was without a lover and instead relied upon her women friends for connection and support. She continued the breathing and meditation practices she had cultivated on her own early in her life. Her journaling practice expanded into an artistic mix of words, images, dreams, and musings. Gradually, her loneliness subsided as her self-esteem and supportive friendships blossomed. We decided this was a good time for her to take a break from therapy.

Six months later, Carolyn came for a follow-up appointment. She told me, "I recently began dating a kind, generous, single guy. I met him at a dinner party that one of my college friends organized. He's different from the kind of man I usually date. There's no drama. In fact, Garret is somewhat reserved, but he makes me laugh and feel safe. I'm optimistic about him, but at the same time I want to move things along slowly, so that there are no surprises. My friends have been great in supporting me through this early dating phase."

Carolyn's journaling became a vehicle for her creativity that had long gone untapped. She regularly built in time for her girlfriends, who became a great source of strength and joy. Carolyn moved past the wounds of her childhood, and with time and practice she overcame her perpetual feelings of loneliness and isolation. In their place, she built genuine, loving relationships that nourished her deeply.

CHAPTER FOUR
Disconnection from Family

Molly

Molly, an attractive, fifty-six-year-old, accomplished executive and married mother of two, was suddenly no longer able to maintain the delicate balance between the demands of her career and family life. She worked for a successful venture capital firm while her husband, Jeffrey, traveled frequently for his job. Out of necessity Molly had become a "superwoman," single-handedly caring for their adopted daughters—Ali, sixteen, and Chloe, fourteen—while working long hours.

Her world began to unravel one evening when she discovered empty beer cans and a vodka bottle, along with a couple of condoms, in the trash. It was clear where the evidence pointed, and Molly immediately wondered what else Ali, and possibly Chloe, might be involved in. She went into high gear to investigate the situation. As Ali slept, Molly scrolled through the text messages on her phone. What she saw was not the Ali she thought she knew.

The texts and the in-your-face partying evidence blindsided Molly. Her shock swiftly morphed into guilt that she had been neglecting her girls. How could she not have noticed the signs that Ali and possibly Chloe were drinking and having sex? Sure, Ali had started dressing provocatively, but that was the style her peers were wearing. Chloe did seem to be losing her focus at school and was a little withdrawn at home, but Molly had assumed that was just part of adjusting to a competitive high school. The more she thought about it, the more concerned Molly became that she really had no idea what her girls' day-to-day lives were like. The texting and sexting she had uncovered on Ali's phone seemed to prove that she didn't even know who her girls' friends were. All of a sudden, Molly felt like she had failed her daughters. Even worse, she saw her window of opportunity to influence Ali and Chloe before they headed off to college slipping through her fingers.

Uncharacteristically, Molly made a swift decision: she decided to take a six-month leave of absence from work to become a full-time, stay-at-home mom. The fallout from this sudden shift in her professional life, coupled with the frightening issues facing her girls, catapulted Molly into my office.

Sex, Drugs, and Rock and Roll

At our first meeting, Molly explained, "A few months ago, I noticed that Ali had started wearing makeup and wearing more revealing clothes. I didn't think much of it and just discouraged her from exposing too much skin. Then, as I told you over the phone, I found the empty alcohol bottles, the condoms, and the sexting photos. That was it. I panicked and couldn't stand the thought that I'd failed to know Ali was in trouble and maybe I had been neglecting both my girls. It didn't help that Ali was blaming me for 'ruining her life' and screaming obscenities at me because we grounded her. I still can't believe I took a leave from my job so fast, but I did. I just had to straighten everything out so we could get back to the life we thought we knew.

"Everything deteriorated so quickly. About a month ago, Ali was caught smoking pot on school grounds when she was supposed to be in class. She got suspended from school for a week, and Jeffrey and I grounded her for a month. What a joke. Try grounding a sixteen-year-old who's sneaky, lies to you, and has older friends who have their own cars and show up with their lights off to pick her up at two o'clock in the morning for some 'recreation.' Jeffrey and I have tried to talk some sense into her, but she just screams at us and slams the door to her room.

"Last week, I got a call from the school counselor only to find out that Chloe had skipped a couple of classes, and the counselor thinks she may be depressed. Chloe had been acting kind of apathetic at home, but nothing I thought was a real problem. She used to be my bubbly girl, but not anymore. I managed to persuade her to go to therapy because she wouldn't talk to me and I was terrified she would soon start to follow in her sister's footsteps, if she hadn't already. But I don't think therapy is doing much good, because it's been a battle getting her to go each week. She's so mad at me and just gives me 'the look' and rolls her eyes, which drives me crazy!

"I have no idea how or why everything is suddenly falling apart with my girls. Things used to be so predictable, and now nothing is, and it feels like it never will be again. Jeffrey and I thought we were doing a good job managing our girls and our work. We were all so happy. I just don't understand what happened."

"What don't you understand?" I asked.

Flustered and drawing in a deep breath, Molly explained, "Chloe and Ali have these secret lives. It's like I don't know them at all anymore. They don't want to talk with Jeffrey or me. I feel like I've been this terrible mother, that I missed something major and that their problems are my fault. I don't understand how I could have been so oblivious.

"I know Jeffrey is responsible, too, but it feels like my fault and my problem. He doesn't worry like I do. He thinks everything will turn out fine, and that they are just being teenagers. Jeffrey sees their antics as just a passing phase. I don't agree, and that's causing some friction between us. Getting the girls back on track is my job, but it feels like unknown territory to me. For the first time in my life, I'm facing something I totally don't know how to do, let alone how to do well."

Molly struck me as an intelligent, caring mother and an ambitious woman. Her identity had been tied primarily to her work for over thirty years. She considered herself a "superwoman" in her executive capacity. While Molly loved her daughters, she felt less empowered and more tentative in her role as a mother. She felt she needed to slow down and shift her focus from her high-powered professional life to become more actively involved with her children, particularly during their adolescent years.

The "Good Enough" Mother

Molly needed to find a way to take better care of herself during this major transition. For the past few years she had been running herself ragged managing work and home, and did virtually nothing for her own self-care. In recent years she had stopped working out, taking time to garden, or doing any of the activities she used to love. Becoming a full-time mom was going to be a major life adjustment. This change meant, at least temporarily, giving up a job in which she felt highly competent, and transitioning to the role of full-time mother in which she felt insecure, at best. I assured Molly that she possessed everything necessary to make this shift. She continued to struggle deeply with feelings of guilt and now believed that her absence during her daughters' earlier years might have damaged them in some way.

Feelings of guilt and loss are common for mothers, regardless of the path chosen. The ubiquitous question "Am I a 'good enough' mother?" is pondered by moms who choose to stay home to care for their children full-time, as well as those who choose to work outside of the home full-time or part-time. The answer to this question often proves to be painfully elusive, as it was for Molly.

Molly had been a thoughtful and attentive mother all along, and she needed to embrace this truth. The fact that Ali and Chloe were experimenting with some risky behaviors was of legitimate concern, but not far from the norm for many adolescents. However, I did agree with Molly that she needed to be more available to her daughters now and help them make better choices regarding their health and safety. I observed that Molly was unusually hard on herself. In our initial work together, I sensed that her preoccupation with guilt interfered with her ability to be present for her daughters. Before Molly would be able to improve her communication with them, she needed to become more compassionate with herself and develop the understanding that she was a "good enough" mom.

D. W. Winnicott coined the term "good enough mother" in the early 1950s. He was a British pediatrician and psychoanalyst who studied the mother-infant relationship. He described the "ordinary devoted mother" as one who is able to establish a loving relationship with her baby by sensing and satisfying his or her needs. Winnicott explained that while a mother does not always read these signals correctly, she does so often enough for the infant's healthy growth and development. In this sense, Winnicott validated that no mother can be perfect, but most mothers are "good enough." Additional research has confirmed that "mini-failures" of attunement are, in fact, necessary for a baby's development as they create opportunities for the infant to learn to self-soothe.

Today, with women's roles expanding and becoming more complex, the struggle to find work-life balance has become a significant challenge. Now more than ever, the idea of "good enough" has great relevance and can serve as an important and comforting reminder that not only is perfection an illusion, but ultimately it does not support our children in their efforts to move toward successful independence. We must learn to accept being good enough in all the roles we assume—mother, daughter, partner, and professional. Sometimes we are required to give more of our energy to one aspect of our lives than another, and then, invariably, the demands shift and we must adjust. By learning to accept our limitations we become more self-aware and more self-compassionate. We are also better able to accept the imperfections of our children, partners, and colleagues. This is a great gift to the people in our lives.

To better understand the current situation, I felt it would be useful to learn more about Molly's history. I asked Molly to tell me about her background. She took me back to her courtship with Jeffrey.

"After about four years of dating, Jeffrey and I decided to marry. We'd spent years building our careers in New York. Both of our companies had divisions in Boston and offered us promotions, so we moved. We thought the lifestyle might be less stressful in the suburbs. I'd always focused exclusively on my career, never quite sure if I wanted to have children. Then, to my surprise, I turned thirty-six and suddenly realized that I really wanted a child, a family of my own. At the same time, I was always ambitious and loved the recognition I received at work, so I planned to go back to the job shortly after having my baby and just scale back a bit."

"Sounds like a good plan. So what happened?"

"I was ready to have my baby. Unfortunately, my body wasn't. Over the next few years, I had three miscarriages and all kinds of tests, procedures, and several rounds of in vitro fertilization. Every time I got pregnant I would get so excited and hopeful, just to have my heart broken into a million pieces with each miscarriage. No one besides Jeffrey and my parents knew the extent of my anguish. The hormonal fluctuations were brutal.

"Jeffrey and I kept trying. I'd always succeeded at everything and was determined to make this happen, too. As I got closer to forty, I realized this probably was not going to happen. I cried all the time and couldn't think of anything else. Jeffrey would have been okay without children, but I was not. My longing for a child just didn't quiet down. We decided to adopt and ended up going through an agency. Almost a year later, our beautiful Ali arrived."

"Was adoption a difficult decision for you?"

"Not really, once I'd accepted that I couldn't have a child of my own. In the end, it didn't matter. I fell madly in love with Ali, and then two years later, with Chloe. I don't think I could have loved them more if I'd given birth to them myself.

"Ali was my blond-haired, blue-eyed cherub. As much as I cherished our time together, after my six-month parental leave I felt compelled to get back to work. I missed feeling like the expert, I missed the income, and I longed for the adult contact. I think, in hindsight, I was lonely. Jeffrey was always traveling, and I thought that with great childcare we'd have the best of both worlds. Although I cut back my hours, I still felt pangs of regret about leaving Ali. At the same time, I felt like a prisoner staying home full-time. It was crazy-making. I was never quite settled either way, but I just shoved down my feelings and moved on, like I always had.

"When we adopted Chloe two years later, our family felt complete. I did a better job of handling 'the balance' without all the guilt and confusion. I took another six months off, but as much as I loved my girls, I just wasn't happy being home full-time and returned to work. Again, the guilt kicked in. Perhaps it was selfish of me, but I needed the adult contact and we didn't want to give up the income and the lifestyle it afforded us. Loneliness and the 'golden handcuffs' seduced me back into work."

Sadly, many women feel guilt around trying to find the balance between work and raising children. The truth is that there is no real balance. There is no perfection. We can only do the best that we can do. Many of us feel guilty about not being available to our children when we are at work and guilty about our work when we are with our children. Although working and raising a family can be compatible, many of us feel the tug of guilt regardless of our choices even when there are no warning signs.

Engaging in mindfulness exercises like meditation, breath work, or journaling can help to gain clarity and perspective on the situation. Molly had enough self-awareness to understand that she needed to learn skills to calm down and let go of her self-critical, guilt-inducing thoughts. She had never practiced any mindfulness strategies but was a willing candidate. I taught her the breathing, meditation, and affirmation exercises, just as I had with Anne, and she began to take control of the intensity of her emotional world. She felt more available to her girls. Sharing her story with me was particularly important for Molly right now, as she no longer had a support network from her work environment.

Healthy and Unhealthy Guilt

Guilt is a complicated emotion that gives us important information about a behavior or a decision we have made. Its purpose is to alert us that we did something wrong, and to help us develop a better sense of our behavior. There are healthy and unhealthy forms of guilt. Healthy guilt is our moral compass because it allows us to examine our behavior, learn from it, and take appropriate measures to change our actions going forward. Healthy guilt helps us protect our relationships. It signals to us that we have hurt or let down a friend, a colleague, or a loved one. We then pay closer attention to our behavior so that we can safeguard these important relationships. We are all fallible, but once we address the behavior that led to the feeling of guilt, we are poised to let go of this painful feeling. The same is true of meeting our responsibilities. We feel guilty when we shirk them, and this leads us to take the actions necessary to fulfill our obligations.

Unhealthy guilt is a nagging, persistent feeling that contributes to low self-esteem and depression. We feel bad about behaviors and decisions without understanding why. Unhealthy guilt goes unexpressed and unexamined, and usually stems from some earlier unresolved conflict. It serves no purpose and does not result in greater self-knowledge. There is no identifiable mistake, yet the guilt continues to make us feel bad about ourselves. We beat ourselves up for perceived failings and find it impossible to let go of these awful feelings so we can move on. Unhealthy guilt is difficult to resolve because there is no particular behavior to understand or change. Professional help is advisable if this feeling does not eventually resolve.

Molly's experience of guilt was the healthy sort, signaling to her to pay closer attention to her daughters. For now, being available to Ali and Chloe was the best path for Molly.

"Molly," I said, "guilt is a complicated and painful emotion that occurs when you make choices that are out of sync with your core values. The purpose of guilt is to let you know when a decision you have made feels wrong. It's your signal to examine your choices head-on so that you can adjust accordingly, and this is exactly what you have done. Staying home full-time is not an easy transition for you to make; however, the teenage years are a particularly complex time in your daughters' lives. Being with your girls now will serve them well. I suspect you will also find that your guilt will quiet down."

Strategy for Managing Guilt

- Identify the nature of your guilt. Is there a message to glean from the guilt, or is it an irrational response? Differentiate between healthy and unhealthy guilt. Notice what you feel guilty about. Examples of healthy guilt: "I need to spend more time with my children." "I need to stop getting angry at my elderly mother when she repeats herself." Examples of unhealthy guilt: "Why do I always say such stupid things?" "I am a bad person." Focus particular attention on what is behind the guilt in your relationships.

- Make amends or behavioral changes. Once you identify the behavior that makes you feel guilty, it clarifies what you need to do to repair or change the situation. The sooner the behavioral changes are made, the sooner the guilt will dissipate and your self-esteem will improve.

- Accept that you made a mistake and move on. Once you make amends for past inappropriate or hurtful behavior, forgive yourself and move on. Learn from the past and let it inform the future.

- Recognize that guilt carries with it a message that demands our attention. Usually, guilt motivates us to change a behavior and to become more aware, more present, and more compassionate.

Navigating Through a Difficult Transition

Molly sat silently, lost in thought. Finally, she said, "This is hard, much harder than I thought it would be. I need you to help me reach Ali and Chloe."

I asked her to tell me more about when the girls were young.

"Ali was my easy child. She was quiet, good-natured, and playful. Ali cooed, laughed, and loved snuggling. Jeffrey and I adored her from the moment we laid eyes on her. At first, when the babysitter came and I had to leave her for work, it was painful to let go and have someone else witness some of her 'firsts.' Over time, I got used to it. For Jeffrey, the childcare piece didn't even register. He hadn't felt the anguish of the miscarriages, the procedures, and the ultimate realization that I would never have my own children, not that it mattered in the end. When Ali finally came to us, I felt this intense love I had never known before.

"Ali's first birthday was the day Jeffrey and I decided we wanted another child, even though there was already never enough time in the day. We were so happy with Ali and thought another baby would round out our family. Within a year, after jumping through many hoops, we finally got our baby girl. Unlike Ali, Chloe cried and fussed all day long. I thought I was losing my mind. With no one to talk to and the constant crying, work beckoned me. Nevertheless, I felt awful leaving my girls."

Molly choked up, quickly collected herself, and continued to explain. She said, "My colleagues at work were my friends and support system. I missed them terribly. I missed the challenges, the intensity of the deals, the ups and downs of the industry; the whole thing made me come to life. I liked being the expert and feeling in control. None of that came with being a mother. Now that I'm home again, I find myself vacillating between feeling anxious about the girls and depressed about my loss of identity. I've got to come to terms with my commitment to being home so I can give them my best self, not this mixed-up, depressed version of me. This is why I'm here."

Molly sat silently for a moment. I assured her that she would be able to help her daughters and herself. She needed to continue talking about her feelings and learn strategies to manage this unknown territory. I thought that in addition to understanding how her own history might be influencing her experience, it would be helpful to spend more time on the breath work and internalizing some affirmations. Molly needed to better tolerate or minimize her fears and concerns as she navigated through this difficult transition. She began meditating twice a day, first in the morning and then before the girls came home from school.

We spent several sessions discussing her feelings about deciding to become a mother. She was the only daughter of an old-fashioned and domineering father who desperately tried to control his daughter. He believed that a woman's place was at home, raising children, and caring for her family. Not surprisingly, Molly's mother was a full-time homemaker and never questioned her role. Her charismatic and narcissistic father had serial affairs, and her mom remained seemingly oblivious to his periodic absences. Molly thought he might have fathered other children. She vowed never to become subservient like her mother, and she became quite determined professionally. Tragically, Molly's parents died in a car accident when her daughters were very young and, until now, she had never attempted to resolve her complicated feelings toward them. Her work was to develop insight, forgive her "imperfect" parents, and become mindful about the way she chose to parent her daughters.

I suggested to Molly, "By choosing to work, you showed your daughters a path that your parents hadn't offered to you. You've given your girls a great example of a good marriage with two accomplished parents and an empowered mom who has helped raise the glass ceiling."

Molly appreciated my encouragement, but still felt like she'd "missed it" somehow. I asked her to explain. She said, "I just feel like I've wasted so much time proving myself and that I should have been more available to my daughters all these years. I've been beating myself up about the choices I've made. Jeffrey tells me I have been a good mother, but I don't feel that way because Ali and Chloe are not okay right now, and if I'd really been a good mother they would not be acting out this way."

"Molly, I think you need to say good-bye to what you perceive as past mistakes," I encouraged. "Let them go, so you can be more fully present to your girls now. You need to know that your instincts are spot-on and this is a good time to devote yourself to them." We sat together for a few silent moments, which seemed more pensive than awkward.

I thought a heart-centered breathing strategy would help Molly manage the cascade of emotions—both past and present—that she was experiencing.

Heart-Centered Breathing

I suggested we take several abdominal breaths and then move on to another phase of breath work. I told Molly to place one of her hands over her heart center. "Allow the air to fill your belly and then rise into your chest cavity, your heart space. Feel the expansion in your chest and heart and let in the thought, *I am compassionate with myself and accept what is right now*. Visualize the expansion of your heart as you practice. For the first few minutes of this exercise, place one hand on your belly and the other on your heart. This will enhance your experience of heart-centered breathing."

Molly's homework assignment was to practice this method of breathing for five to ten minutes, once or twice a day, with the intention of relaxing her mind and body while opening up her heart. I encouraged her to visualize this process as she breathed. After a week of practice, I suggested that as she "opened her heart space," she visualize forgiving herself and her parents for any mistakes they made in the past.

Heart-Centered Breathing Practice

- Sit in a comfortable position.
- Take a few abdominal breaths to relax mind and body.
- Allow your breath to fill your belly and then rise into your chest cavity.
- Visualize the breath filling your heart space.
- Feel the expansion in your chest and heart.
- Focus on the thought, *I am compassionate with myself and accept what is right now.*
- Continue this practice for five to ten minutes.
- Notice how you feel.

Molly responded well to this exercise. Alternating between breath work and meditation, she began to let go of years of hurt. She felt more self-compassion and began to forgive her parents for their weaknesses, disapproval, and early abandonment. Over the next sessions, we continued to talk about Molly's past and the power of affirmations.

Affirmations to Create Positive Change

Many of us begin our day with unconscious negativity. While getting ready in the morning, it is not uncommon for a woman to look in the mirror and immediately think thoughts like *My skin looks lousy, I look tired, I'll never get through this day, I look fat.* These thoughts contribute mightily to the way we feel about ourselves and set a negative tone for the day. Our thought patterns can either sabotage us or foster possibilities. By intentionally replacing the thought *I am anxious* with something positive, such as *I am excited,* we cultivate a more positive perspective.

Research confirms that our thoughts activate different parts of the brain. That is, distinct neurological changes occur along with our thoughts. Whatever thoughts we choose to focus on become stronger and eventually shape our inner experience. Therefore, it behooves us to become mindful of the thoughts we are effectively choosing to reinforce.

Affirmations are simple, positive self-statements or suggestions to focus on that are based in truth or are within the realm of possibility. An affirmation can be a word, phrase, or sentence that reflects a positive perspective on a thought, behavior, characteristic, or one's overall state of being. When we are in a relaxed state of mind and repeat an affirmation, that suggestion finds its way into a deep place in our consciousness. When relaxed, we are more receptive to suggestion, so it is particularly important to be mindful of how we speak to ourselves under these circumstances. For example, in the morning before you even get out of bed, think about some positive aspect of the day. This tends to establish a more optimistic context for your day.

Molly had internalized the negative voice of her parents and judged herself harshly as a mother. She cared deeply about her daughters and had always done her best for them, but she never felt good enough as a mom because she had chosen to work full-time. The reality was that only in the past year had the girls begun to show signs of trouble, and even then their behavior was within the scope of normal experimental adolescent behavior. Molly went so far as to leave her job at the peak of her career so she could be there for them when she sensed they might be in danger. These were all things a loving, caring mother would do.

At one of our sessions Molly said, "I want to create an affirmation about the guilt I feel about having neglected my girls and not being a good mother. I know intellectually that this is not the case, but my mind keeps cycling back to this dark place." She was beginning to realize that whenever she repeated negative or self-deprecating thoughts, she reinforced this negativity and the associated painful feelings. I suggested that when thoughts like these came to mind, she replace them with the affirmation "I am a good, loving, and competent mother." These words resonated with her, but she had not yet become secure in their message. I knew that with practice her perspective about herself as a mother would shift and become more positive. I suggested that after a few deep abdominal breaths or at the end of each meditation session, she repeat the affirmation to herself, visualizing herself as a good and competent mother.

Although affirmations create a potent vehicle for shifting the brain from a pessimistic perspective to an optimistic one, it is important to note that they cannot erase the negative messages we received in childhood. However, affirmations do allow us to build a repertoire of positive thoughts that can ultimately become more potent and prominent in our minds.

Molly had been magnifying her self-perception as a bad mother through her own persistent negative self-talk. She needed to understand the many subliminal ways she wove these negative thoughts into her daily existence. Once aware of how pervasive these thoughts were, she became better equipped to interrupt this destructive pattern. As negative thoughts presented themselves, she would take notice, but would not focus on them. She would take some deep breaths and repeat her affirmation to counter the negativity. The affirmation statement or phrase did not need to be perfectly true, just within the realm of possibility. Molly's objective was to train her brain to develop a more positive perspective. Over time, she became less harsh and judgmental in her relationship with herself and her daughters. Molly began to feel like she finally had some control over the negative voice within.

The "How" of Affirmations

- Create a simple, positive phrase or statement about yourself.
- Write your affirmation down on a Post-it or in a journal.
- Sit in a comfortable position.
- Take slow, deep, rhythmic, abdominal breaths.
- Allow your mind and body to relax.
- Repeat your affirmation several times to yourself and visualize yourself in that context.
- When negative thoughts intrude, bring your attention back to your affirmation.
- Practice often.

When you feel the effects of your practiced affirmation, you are ready to move on to another area in your life that needs attention. Create another simple, positive affirmation. Over time, you can build a personalized library of affirmations. Practice your affirmations when you find your mind drifting into the negative or whenever you are looking for a boost in matters of self-esteem, love, work, and health. Always begin by taking some deep breaths and relaxing the mind and body. Journaling about your affirmations will allow you to track your progress.

The breathing, brief meditations, affirmations, and deepening insight seemed to help Molly feel more empowered in her new role. She now had several strategies to use in her daily life when self-doubt or fear emerged. She created an array of affirmations such as *I am brave, I am wise, I am beautiful,* and *my girls are safe and healthy, and they will thrive in life.*

Molly regularly practiced and visualized experiencing greater harmony with Ali and Chloe, and they were safe. As predicted, her mind began to shift away from the negative and scary thoughts to a more positive perspective.

For many women, being present and being mindful are critical tools for getting through a tough transition. I suggested to Molly, "In the past, your energy has enabled you to juggle a busy career and family life. Now it's important to slow down, focus, and use that energy to connect with your family in a meaningful way."

Her greatest fear remained that her girls were putting themselves in harm's way. Molly said she sometimes slipped into prayer during or after the practice of her affirmations, which was another powerful way of seeking support and finding her way during this challenging time. "I'm committed to doing whatever it takes to connect with them. I just have to give this my best shot and know that I will not turn into my father's domineering clone or lose my own identity the way my mother did."

"Getting" Adolescence

Molly practiced her affirmations and expanded them to include positive statements about her relationship with Jeffrey. She noted, "For the first time in my life, I can manage my fear and guilt. I can't believe that such a small shift in my thinking can make such a big difference in the way I feel.

"Jeffrey continues to travel, and can only spend time with us on the weekends. It's a challenge for him to understand Ali and Chloe, and I think the stress around the house really gets to him. I feel so alone trying to figure out how to deal with them. I am extremely focused on them, but I know that it would be so much better if I had a few good friends in the community. It would help me sort out what is normal behavior for girls their age and what is destructive. I don't know where to begin in my search for support."

"I agree that you need to develop more of a network of friends," I said. I know that will happen for you in due time, and we can certainly discuss this in greater detail. For now, let's take stock of the situation. Clearly, Ali is experimenting with drugs and sex, and Chloe might be as well. Your job right now is to keep a vigilant eye on them and set some boundaries, without being too overbearing. Some of the questions to consider with regard to the girls are: Have you noticed changes in their behavior other than the ones we have already discussed? Does Ali or Chloe isolate herself? Does either of them seem depressed or self-injurious? Suicidal? These are the sorts of things you need to pay close attention to."

Molly shook her head decidedly and said she had not observed any such changes in their behavior.

"Other than that, it is normal for the girls to begin separating from you and Jeffrey and connecting more with their peers. Of course, this period can be stormy and cause a great deal of stress in the family. Their friends are probably experimenting in similar ways, and it would certainly be helpful for you to connect with other parents to share experiences. Perhaps you can get involved with the PTO, the school committee, or fund-raising events so that you can get a pulse on what's going on with other kids. However, the best way to find out what Ali and Chloe are up to is to improve your communication with them."

Molly agreed, but added anxiously, "I don't know where to begin. They both seem so impenetrable." I assured Molly that we would find a way together. I reminded her that serious intervention with her daughters needed to occur only when their health and safety were at risk. The challenge for now was for Molly to continue monitoring their behavior for red flags such as significant shifts in appearance, unusual secrecy or absences, or excessive argumentativeness or moodiness. Maintaining ongoing connection and dialogue is vital during this phase of teenage development.

For the first time, Molly felt good about her decision to take a break from her career and step into the trenches of her children's adolescence. Several months later she resigned from her job, planning to not return to work until Chloe graduated from high school. Molly committed full-out to improving her self-care, developing greater mindfulness, and improving her ability to communicate so she could give her daughters her best. Each morning after the girls left for school, she faithfully exercised or took a brisk walk outside when the weather permitted. After that, she came home and did her twenty-minute mindfulness regimen. That one precious hour of personal time gave her the fortitude and insight she needed to navigate through her day.

As a next step, I suggested to Molly that we talk more in-depth about communicating with her girls. I knew she was a skilled communicator in the work arena, but I thought some coaching regarding her approach with Ali and Chloe might be useful.

Better Communication

Active listening is essential for building and maintaining healthy relationships. Much of our day involves listening to our partners, children, colleagues, bosses, or clients. If you listen well, people will be drawn to you. They will want to share their stories with you and your relationships will become stronger. A statement widely attributed to Maya Angelou speaks to this sentiment: "I've learned that people will forget what you said, people will forget what you did, but people will never forget how you made them feel."

How you make them feel is based on your ability to listen carefully and compassionately. When others feel truly heard, connection happens, even when a difference of opinion exists. Listening to another conveys to the person speaking that she is valued. Feeling valued helps us to heal and grow strong. Molly's girls needed to feel seen and heard by their mom.

Active listening is one of the most powerful ways to improve listening skills. When you make a conscious effort to pay close attention to the message, meaning, tone, and nuances of the speaker's words, you are listening actively. Active listening and thoughtfully responding to another deepens mutual understanding. Often when we speak with one another, we become distracted or we begin to think about our own responses rather than tuning in to the speaker. We assume we understand the other person without being mindful and checking to see if our assumptions are valid.

The active listener focuses on the words and gestures of the speaker in a wholehearted way, keeping interference from cell phones or your own associations to a minimum. The listener indicates her engagement by giving subtle cues like nodding or saying, "I understand," or "That must be difficult." It often helps to clarify your perception of the conveyed message by *reframing* or repeating in a different way what you think the speaker communicated. The technique of reframing allows the speaker to discover whether mutual understanding has taken place. The speaker may then have the opportunity to clarify or refine the intended message.

With reframing, the listener reiterates the meaning of the communication and, perhaps, the associated feeling state. For example, the speaker explains that she needs help with a particular problem. Instead of simply repeating the message, the active listener might acknowledge the speaker's feeling state: "I'm sorry that you are hurt, angry, sad, disappointed, etc." This observation deepens the speaker's experience of feeling understood and strengthens the connection between speaker and listener. When the speaker feels visible, understood, and valued, the relationship between the listener and the speaker is strengthened even when disagreement exists.

I shared some observations with Molly: "Making the transition from full-time corporate life to full-time mom has probably created feelings of loss and resentment. You might not always be aware of the way these feelings creep into your behavior and conversations. Stepping back and taking a few deep breaths can help you notice if this is happening, bring you into the moment, and remind you to listen better. To repair your relationship with Ali and Chloe, you may need to take your feelings and needs out of the equation, and focus on what they are trying to communicate.

"When you are having a conversation with either of them, pay close attention to the content of what they say and the way in which they communicate it to you. Do your best to withhold judgment, and just listen. Ask them relevant questions for clarification and give small signs to indicate that you are listening wholeheartedly. A nod, a short phrase like 'That must have been hard' lets them know that you are trying to connect.

"Abdominal breathing is the secret weapon that supports you in staying calm and remaining present as you listen to difficult messages. Particularly when emotions are running high, remind yourself to breathe and concentrate on the message being conveyed. Active listening without judgment will draw Ali and Chloe closer to you.

"The truth is, most of us don't feel understood the way we would like, and this is especially true in adolescence. Chloe and Ali are probably both feeling misunderstood and unheard. With their teenage brains still developing, these feelings are greatly amplified. Improving your capacity to listen will connect you more deeply with them and give you greater insight into what is going on with them.

"Let your girls know that whatever they share with you will not be a deal breaker for your relationship. You can handle whatever they tell you. If they believe that it is safe to talk to you, they will be more likely to open up. It is important for them to know that you are willing to go the distance with them."

Active Listening

- Pay attention to verbal and nonverbal messages. Give the speaker your undivided attention. Look directly at the speaker. Breathe when you start to lose focus.

- Use body language and gestures to show that you are listening. Make eye contact, nod, smile, interject with "uh-huh" or "I understand" when appropriate.

- Reframe, reflect, and paraphrase the delivered message. Comments like "It sounds like you are saying . . ." or "What I am hearing is . . ." help to clarify the communication.

- Tone trumps content. Regardless of what someone is saying, the most important message is being delivered through tone of voice rather than the content of what is said.

- Give the speaker space and suspend judgment. Allow the speaker to communicate the message without interruption— unless interruption is essential for your understanding.

- Avoid the word *but* as much as possible. *But* is a word that tends to negate everything the person said just prior to it.

- Respond to the speaker with compassion and authenticity. Even a strong message can be delivered kindly. Think about how you would feel hearing your own message.

- Be patient and breathe. With regular practice, you can improve your active-listening skills. It takes time to train your brain to remain focused.

I said to Molly, "For the next few weeks, I'd like for you to concentrate on carefully listening to everything Ali and Chloe tell you. Listen for the meaning and nuances of what they are saying. Try to minimize your expectations of their ability to understand you. During adolescence, narcissism is at an all-time high. They probably do not see your perspective. Notice what happens when they see that you are really interested in what they have to say."

Mindful Listening

We discussed the subtleties of active or mindful listening. "Consider it a form of meditation to listen to your girls. Look at them and connect with your eyes. Let them express their thoughts and ideas, without criticizing. Rephrase their messages to make sure you've heard them accurately. If you didn't get it quite right, let them clarify their thoughts. Even when you disagree with what either of them is saying, they will feel valued if you give them this kind of attention. Remember that *tone trumps content*. The way they are telling you something is often more important than the actual words they use. The same holds true for your responses to them.

"Think carefully about the way you speak to them. Remember that the way you deliver your message matters. So take a few breaths, ground yourself, and speak to them from a calm and thoughtful perspective. Treat them respectfully and recognize that they are in the process of developing their own unique worldview. Use 'I' statements. For example, instead of telling Ali, 'You are so disrespectful when you don't tell me where you are going,' consider saying, 'I worry about you when I don't know where you are.' The first example puts your daughter on the defensive, and the second one focuses on your love and concern for her.

"When you say 'no,' explain why. Your daughters need to feel that your responses to them are not just autocratic and automatic. Their health and safety are the best reasons to feel secure in denying a request.

"Create some pleasurable rituals for spending time together, such as going out for coffee, lunch, or a movie. These are stress-free ways to devote some time exclusively to each daughter. When you create sweet opportunities to be with Ali and Chloe individually, they will probably open up in surprising ways, without feeling forced or cajoled."

Active Listening Works

Molly embraced these communication strategies, although letting go of her tendency to dominate or control the course of the conversation was not easy. She experimented with her approach over the next several weeks. The first thing she said on any given day was not about something they needed to do or something they did wrong. She greeted them, asked about their day, listened to their answers, and closely monitored her tone. Molly asked questions out of concern and curiosity, and then paid careful attention to their answers. She discovered that, gradually, they became more willing to talk—especially as they realized that she was not going to criticize or threaten them with consequences. She gave them more space to make their own decisions, as long as their health and safety were not being compromised.

During one session, Molly shared an insight into her relationship with Chloe. "She had been tuning me out over the past year because she felt like I wasn't interested in her life and didn't care about her feelings. She called me out for not knowing the names of her friends and missing some school events. Chloe said that until now my only conversation with her was to remind her about chores and responsibilities at home or school. I realized she was dead-on. That's exactly what I had done. Chloe had been competing with my work for attention and losing the battle, so she decided to pull away from me. Ditching her classes and withdrawing from me was her way of getting my attention."

In the months that followed, Molly worked hard to refine her listening skills. "Chloe realizes I've been trying to connect with her. I'm trying to assume the best and trust her, which seems to be working well. She seems more like her old happier self, and her grades have improved. Reminding myself to breathe and listening actively have made a huge difference in being able to be present when spending time with each of them.

"Even Ali has been more talkative. She stopped smoking pot and cigarettes. I didn't even know about the cigarettes! Jeffrey and I are more on the same page now, too. We're both still concerned that there's been alcohol at some of the recent parties we've let her attend. Now that she is being open with us, we know that she won't drink and drive, or get into a car with someone who has been drinking. It's interesting to me that now that we've given her a little more room to experiment, she's been acting out less. I think she feels like we are trusting her more and not trying to control her as much. Last weekend, she and a friend chose to leave a party that seemed to be getting a bit wild. They were right. The police showed up an hour later and now some of Ali's lacrosse teammates are suspended from the team. It made her consider consequences in a new way, and she felt good about making the choice to leave early and not drink. I'm amazed that she even told us about that party. She would not have done so six months ago.

"I'm taking Ali shopping next weekend for a dress because she just got invited to the senior prom. My hope is that we can talk more about her friendships and relationships with boys. I plan to share with her how hard my teenage years were for me and maybe some of the choices I regret. Obviously, I can never bring up what I found on her phone, but maybe she'll be willing to talk about what's going on with the senior she's dating. He seems okay, but Jeffrey and I want to get to know him better. We asked Ali to find a time to invite him over for a casual dinner. That might be pushing it, but we'll see. I just want her to feel supported by Jeffrey and me, and know that we stand behind her no matter what. Most of all, I really look forward to our time together."

Molly continued to tell me how she'd found herself being "more in the moment" with her daughters and more relaxed during her alone time. She accepted that Ali and Chloe had their own friends and lives, although they seemed glad she was around. Over time, Molly gradually let go of her guilt and embraced the wisdom of being a "good enough mother," giving up any illusion of perfection.

Over the months, Molly and I continued to talk about her thoughts, dreams, and relationships. She began coming early for her appointments so she could walk along the aqueduct near my office and reflect, while practicing abdominal breathing. "I notice that the breathing helps when I go into my dark places," she shared. "Yesterday, I found myself feeling resentment about giving up my work. I took a walk, did some deep breathing, remembered my purpose, and the darkness passed."

Making Peer Connections

Now that things were going more smoothly at home, Molly was starting to address her own social needs. She mentioned, with a hint of sadness, "My closest friends still live in New York where I grew up, and the rest are at my firm. I have a few acquaintances in town, but no real friends. I still feel lonely and isolated with my stay-at-home status." I began talking to Molly about the importance of finding some good women friends, so that her life did not revolve exclusively around the needs of her family.

"You've been talking about feeling lonely and having a sense of loss since leaving your job," I said. "You've made great strides with Ali and Chloe. Remember, this is your time too. You need to develop a few good friendships that will support you during this transition and beyond. You'll be happier and will have even more to offer your family when you feel more fulfilled. Friendships with other women will help you deal with the stressors in your life and bring you more joy." I shared some of the research on the physical and psychological benefits of friends. "You've come to rely on our sessions for conversation and guidance, which is fine. Still, connections outside the office will bring additional support and fun. You can't rely on Jeffrey for regular companionship because of his travel schedule, and besides, as your husband he can only provide a particular kind of support. It's time to start building your 'team' and cultivate friends in your community."

Molly squirmed and sheepishly responded, "I know this is crazy, but I don't relate to full-time mothers. Even though I recently joined their ranks, I'm concerned they aren't particularly interesting."

I suggested, "Rather than being judgmental, why don't you try doing what you've just learned to do with your daughters. Be curious about the other moms, and see what you learn. You might be surprised to find out that there are other smart, sophisticated women in your community. Consider letting some of these women in."

"To be honest, that sounds good, but I feel so vulnerable putting myself out there that way." Molly had established herself as an expert at work, where she had built-in relationships. In her community, she felt neither empowered nor successful. Nevertheless, she needed to venture off her beaten path in search of a few good friends. Feeling superior to other women was her defense against being rejected. Molly had to take some risks if she was going to be successful in establishing friendships. She practiced her heart breathing and affirmations. She would repeat to herself, "I am going to build a great group of friends." The idea of building friendships percolated in her mind for several weeks.

At one of our next sessions, she announced, "I'm going to make at least one phone call a week to a potential friend. I also decided to volunteer for the next fund-raising event at a local hospital. Many women from my neighborhood are involved with this event and I heard that it's a great group of women. Best of all, I just joined a gym where there are regular yoga and spinning classes. I haven't worked out consistently in years." Molly was on her way. Once she started getting to know a few of her peers, she was pleasantly surprised. Molly continued, "The women seem to like me, and they are far more interesting and intelligent than I gave them credit for. I'm ashamed that I had such a critical attitude about them."

Over the next few months, Molly built a small circle of friends and continued working on her relationships with Ali and Chloe. At one of our last sessions, she beamed as she updated me. She shared, "The girls are both doing well in school and our communication has never been better. I'm proud of the young women they are becoming. I started taking Ali out to Starbucks once or twice a week. We agreed that the time we spend together is just for us—no cell phones. It's opened up a stress-free way for us to be together. Chloe and I do something similar, but at a local sandwich shop, her favorite spot in town. I am savoring this time with them."

Reconnecting for Keeps

Molly's life had changed dramatically. She felt truly fortunate, though not without some pangs of loss, about leaving her professional life. Wisely, on occasion, she still got together socially with former colleagues to keep her work connections alive. Molly was clear that time was of the essence for making herself available to her adolescent daughters. Work could wait.

Initially, guilt had been the driving force behind her transition home. Molly came to treasure her time with her daughters. She now had support and an array of strategies, which included breathing, mini-meditations, and affirmations to keep her grounded in the present and able to manage her emotional world. The active-listening strategies improved her communication with family, friends, and colleagues. She opened her mind and heart to new possibilities for her future, and at the same time put to rest the old judgmental narrative of her parents. As

Molly cultivated new friendships in her community, she discovered a surprising sense of joy in these new relationships.

Her wish remained strong for Jeffrey to be around more. In recent months, he had worked to refine some of his own communication skills as a result of Molly's influence. All along, she shared with him the discussions that took place in her therapy, and he bore witness to Molly's positive trajectory with the girls and in her own life. The gap between their parenting styles began to diminish as a result of these conversations. There was a growing sense of ease throughout the household. The girls were more approachable and less volatile, and Molly seemed more relaxed and happy.

Jeffrey's interest in the family dynamics grew and he wanted to be more available for all of his "girls." He promised that after the completion of his current consulting gig, he would not take work engagements that kept him away for more than a few days. Molly had secretly longed for time together as a family and for intimacy with Jeffrey.

She felt grateful for time with Ali and Chloe and anticipated good times ahead with Jeffrey. Molly had begun thinking about starting a part-time, home-based business after Ali left for college in the fall. She assured me, "No rush." Molly was now proud to refer to this time in her life as her "second chance at being a good enough mother."

CHAPTER FIVE
Breakup

Melissa

The ceiling fan whirled softly as Melissa entered my waiting room, her kitten-heeled sandals clicking across the floorboards. In her late thirties, Melissa's mane of cascading auburn hair framed her gorgeous round face. She was dressed casually in a bright-red summer top and khakis, but looked self-conscious as she tugged here and there, adjusting the fit of her clothes while sitting down on the couch.

She and her soon-to-be-ex-husband, Andrew, had been separated and living apart for the past year. Although Melissa and Andrew had spent the last year in couples therapy, her deepest wish for keeping her family together was not to be. Andrew had decided to call it quits and recently moved the rest of his belongings out of their house. As the house was being sold as part of the divorce settlement, Melissa now needed to find an apartment for herself and their two teenage children, Daniel and Jessica, ages sixteen and thirteen, respectively. She was scared, angry, and overcome with grief.

The Agony of Divorce

Melissa needed help moving through and beyond the agony of her divorce and the unraveling of the life she once knew. She desperately wanted to share her story and come to an understanding of why her marriage had come undone. Her anxiety, anger, and grief were palpable, and although she had many friends, she knew that she needed the help of a professional to guide her through the difficult journey that lay ahead. She was aware that she had to let go of the past to rebuild a new life for herself and her children, but she felt paralyzed in her efforts to move forward.

With about half of all first marriages ending in divorce, Melissa's situation was far from uncommon. However, this statistic does not make the pain of divorce any easier to bear. Divorce marks the dissolution of a partnership and of the family unit and, along with it, the end of shared hopes and dreams. Nevertheless, there are skills and strategies that can be learned to aid in the successful navigation of this challenging terrain. This is what I hoped to offer Melissa.

At one of our first sessions, with tears streaming down her face, she whispered, "I don't know that anyone can help, but I've got to talk about the torment that is consuming me. Sometimes I feel like I'm suffocating. Everything seems so dark and hopeless. I can hardly get out of bed in the morning. It feels like someone died. I can't focus on my work, and everything feels empty and meaningless. I mean, except for my children. I cannot believe this is the end. I loved Andrew so.

"Andrew and I were both seventeen when we met on a cross-country teen tour. We were both entering our senior year in high school in towns near each other. Andrew had his driver's license and a sweet little car. He would scoop me up at school, and weekends became ours. He courted me with beautiful picnics in well-chosen spots, walks along the beach, and romantic dinners, and we would make love whenever we could find the privacy. Andrew became my world.

"We were madly in love. He always said our love was forever, and I believed him with all my heart. I saw it in his eyes and felt it in his touch. He was everything I ever dreamed about. Andrew was loyal, smart, and, I thought, my savior."

"What was he saving you from?" I asked.

"I didn't realize it then, but my family was extremely dysfunctional. My mother is now a sober alcoholic, but she drank uncontrollably throughout my childhood. She masked it well until nighttime, and then all bets were off. She's a good person; she just couldn't get control of her addiction. Her own mother was an alcoholic who often ended up in hospitals, mental institutions, and sometimes even jail. Social services took my mother into foster care more than once because of my grandmother's neglect.

"My mother was determined not to be like my grandmother, and she wasn't. She loved and nurtured us, except, of course, when she had been drinking, and then she was out of it, although she was never mean. She cooked delicious meals and spent much of the day making our lives look perfect. Dinnertime was chill time. That's when she would pour vodka in her water glass and not stop drinking until she passed out on the couch. My father inevitably would carry her off to bed.

"My brother and I were on our own in the evenings because she was never fully conscious after dinner. I remember so often just wanting to talk to her or be together, but she simply wasn't 'home.' She was hospitalized a few times and would dry out, but her recovery never lasted—until years later when I was married and had children of my own.

"When my mother was sober, she was awesome, always making everything feel special. She came from a poor family, and she wanted to give us everything that would make us happy. I was her princess and my brother her prince. She bought me beautiful dolls and dressed me in pink, girly clothes, even though I was hardly dainty. My mother loved her family, and I think she did the best she could given her own history. She felt terrible shame about her drinking, but she just couldn't get a grip. I hated that she drank rather than spend time with me, night after night."

Melissa's mother was available part of the day and then vanished into nightly stupors. Deeply attached to her mother, Melissa longed for a more consistent connection. Not surprisingly, early on, Melissa struggled with low self-esteem and eating issues.

"Tell me about your father," I asked.

"My father took extremely good care of my mother and worried about her all the time. She was beautiful and kind, and my father worshipped her. The passion of their relationship ran deep. Occasionally, I heard them making love in the middle of the night. They were very affectionate—like two little 'lovebirds.' He never confronted her about her drinking. I think he was afraid she might leave him if he pressed too hard. The few times my mother was hospitalized, he could hardly function. My father didn't drink; his addictions lay elsewhere. He smoked cigars and played the stock market incessantly. He constantly had his face in the newspaper or on the phone with his broker, checking quotes. He loved us, but didn't make us his priority.

"I know that my father sometimes thought my brother and I obstructed his relationship with my mother. He was madly in love with her. I think he competed with her love for us. My father also saw my weight as a problem. It wasn't anything he said, but at times it felt like he was looking at me with disgust when I ate. By third grade, I remember feeling fat and self-conscious about eating. I began my first diet in fifth grade.

"My younger brother, Eric, began battling drug addiction in his teenage years. I guess we've all wrestled with one addiction or another. By the time Andrew came along, I desperately wanted to cut loose, and he was my escape, my savior. He had no interest in drugs or alcohol. He was dependable and good-natured, and wanted me with all of his heart.

"We married when we were in our early twenties. Our dream wedding, in an elegant hotel overlooking the water with the scent of hundreds of pink and white roses in the air, seemed like a fairy tale. Months before the wedding, my overeating had come to an abrupt halt. For the first time in my memory, I wasn't numbing myself with food. The excess weight melted off my body. The day of the wedding, the tailor sewed my gown right on me and it fit like a second skin. I'd never felt so thin or beautiful.

"A year later, we were living blissfully in our fourth-floor walk-up apartment and I got pregnant. We agreed that I would take care of our baby and home, and Andrew would provide for us and be a good daddy. So, like my mother, without the drinking, I made dinner every night and decorated our apartment, all the while getting bigger and bigger with the pregnancy. The weight felt good and purposeful; we were making a baby.

"I ended up gaining eighty pounds, half of which stayed on months after I delivered Daniel. I was elated with my baby boy and exhausted. I continued eating without thinking much about it, especially since I was nursing. Andrew never mentioned a word about my size; he loved me no matter what. I never considered that there were deeper issues underlying my weight fluctuations.

"I'd taken maternity leave from my marketing job at a local radio station. I liked my work, but we had already decided that I would stay home full-time when my leave ended. Then the company where Andrew was working downsized and he lost his lucrative sales job. We had just put a down payment on a sweet little house in a town with a great school system, and at the zero hour we pulled out of the deal. I was devastated. I kept my feelings to myself, not wanting to make Andrew feel any worse than he already did.

"Andrew kept losing or quitting jobs and each time assigned blame to his bosses, the commute, the unrealistic expectations of the work, and so on. He never thought to look inside himself to understand his perpetual dissatisfaction with work."

In Andrew's pursuit of finding meaningful work, he became more distant and less tuned in to Melissa's needs. The intimacy Melissa desperately sought was drifting away, leaving her to feel lonely and alienated. She tended to her baby and continued to turn to food for comfort, grazing throughout the day and binge eating at night. The compulsive eating numbed Melissa's pain and masked her true desire for a deeper connection.

Compulsive Eating

Compulsive eating is a disorder characterized by continuous or frequent overeating throughout the day. A short period devoted to eating in excess is known as a binge, and for compulsive eaters this does not lead to purging as it does in bulimia. The feeling of a loss of control accompanies this behavior, as do feelings of remorse and guilt in the aftermath. Compulsive eating often leads to weight gain or obesity, but people of any size can have this disorder. Some compulsive eaters will restrict their eating after a binge, until the next time the impulse to overeat strikes.

People eat compulsively for a variety of reasons. Compulsive eating takes on qualities of addiction, and food is used like alcohol or other drugs, gambling, and so on. Loneliness and stress contribute to compulsive eating—or any form of addiction, for that matter. The range of emotions that precipitate a compulsive eating episode is vast. Sadness, anger, shame, anxiety, stress, exhaustion, and boredom can trigger a binge. The hope is that eating will alleviate the painful feelings. Eating may keep the painful emotions away for a short while, but they always come back. Ultimately, stuffing oneself to stifle difficult emotions leads to greater despair and hopelessness. The only way out of this vicious cycle is to become conscious of the feelings that drive the behavior and to develop alternative responses to the experience of these painful emotions. Engaging in psychotherapy is often the best idea with this and other addictive behaviors.

Mindfulness 101

Melissa was not ready to talk about her compulsive eating. She wanted to focus on understanding the demise of her marriage. At the beginning of our next few sessions, I taught her some mindfulness skills to help with her anxiety and increase her ability to manage the emotional upheaval she was experiencing.

She welcomed the idea of learning skills and responded well to abdominal breathing. Melissa immediately felt the calming effects. I advised her to use the breathing several times a day and whenever she noticed herself feeling anxious or going into a dark place. I showed her the constructive-rest position, which would initiate a deeper feeling of relaxation and help her with sleep. Last, I taught her a mini-meditation technique that she could practice in the morning to set the tone for the day and then later in the afternoon, before dealing with children, dinner, and evening activities. Melissa agreed to practice these methods.

The Beginning of the End

At our next session, I asked Melissa about Andrew and when things really began to deteriorate. She told me, "Andrew lost his joie de vivre when he began working in office furniture sales. He hated every minute, but had to stick it out or we wouldn't be able to pay the rent or live decently. He wanted to make me happy. I know he loved me, but Andrew never bothered to learn what I needed emotionally or sexually. He thought he knew it all already, which was a cover for his inadequacies. To be fair, neither of us really knew what the other needed. I don't think I even knew what I needed.

"Andrew withdrew from me sexually and became less interested in our friends. I think he felt out of control, and maybe even a sense of futility. Still, after a miscarriage, I managed to get pregnant with Jessica when Daniel wasn't quite three. We both hoped another child would improve Andrew's depression and our relationship. To my surprise, Andrew announced that he planned to buy us a house, making room for the new baby."

"How were you able to afford that?"

"Andrew went to his mother and asked her for a loan. Although she had witnessed his professional failures, she trusted that he would ultimately succeed at his endeavors—whatever they ended up being. Andrew believed that a beautiful home and the new baby would make him happy. He assured me that we would be okay financially and that I just needed to keep the faith. I kept eating, growing bigger with the pregnancy, and Andrew drifted further away. I thought I had married someone who would save me from my loneliness; instead, I ended up feeling more isolated than ever."

The Repetition Compulsion

Melissa unwittingly married a man who struggled with maintaining intimacy. She longed to connect with Andrew, just as she had longed to connect with her mother. Andrew could not satisfy Melissa's desire for closeness, and again she felt abandoned.

The *repetition compulsion* is a psychological occurrence where a person unconsciously recreates a traumatic past life event in the present. It is often motivated by a wish to master an old injury or rewrite one's personal history, with a happier ending. As children, when a parent is neglectful, we typically believe that the problem lies within us and not with the rejecting or narcissistic parent. The unconscious thought is, if only we could be good enough, we would be worthy of being loved. When suppressed, the painful emotions related to this rejection are stored deep in our memory bank. The repetition compulsion shows itself later in life, when the longing to be loved surfaces and becomes manifest in our current relationships. For example, we unconsciously choose a partner who, like the neglectful parent, cannot adequately satisfy our deepest needs. We relive painful feelings reminiscent of that early relationship and cling to the hope that maybe this time we will secure the love we hunger for. Inevitably, disappointment follows, just as it had for Melissa.

None of us have perfect childhoods, so not surprisingly many of us experience ambivalence or conflicts that interfere with the formation of our best possible relationships. The way out of the repetition compulsion in relationships is to allow the regret and pain of our past to emerge. Healing begins when these feelings are identified and allowed expression. The unmet need for unconditional love that we longed for from our parents must be recognized, grieved, and finally released. Mourning our past disappointments and possibly even forgiving those who hurt us frees us to move forward in our lives. Melissa needed to find a way to let go of the anger and feelings of loss she originally felt with her parents and now experienced again with Andrew.

Over the next several sessions, Melissa continued to talk about her marriage to Andrew and her life with Daniel and Jessica. They were both dedicated and involved parents who were attuned to the needs of their children. Melissa volunteered at the children's school, while working almost full-time, because Andrew's income was so erratic. After work, Andrew coached the kids' baseball and soccer teams. The couple hardly spoke except to coordinate schedules. "We remained oblivious to our marriage slowly falling apart." Melissa's eyes welled up. "I didn't want this. I believed we were forever. I don't know how we drifted so far away from each other. I can't bear losing Andrew and having my family go to pieces. He's given up. I hate that he's really given up."

Melissa's bloodshot eyes overflowed. I urged her to breathe and told her how sorry I was for her pain and loss. I reminded Melissa that her angst would not last forever, but that right now she was going through the worst of it. She continued to weep, yet felt relieved to know that the hurt would not endure. Toward the end of our session, I suggested that after a round or two of abdominal breathing, Melissa repeat to herself the affirmation "Already healed. Already whole." Although she did not feel healed or whole at this point, I knew that repeatedly practicing this statement in a relaxed state of mind would create a more positive framework for Melissa's sense of self.

While the emotional turmoil during the divorce process can be painful, there are ways to successfully manage this experience. Moving through this difficult transition occurs by first noticing emotions as they surface, and then tolerating the feelings of pain and grief that follow. Feelings can emerge quickly, slowly, or unpredictably. It is normal to vacillate between intense feeling states and numbness or depression during this process. Breathing, meditation, and other mindfulness strategies help to quiet, clarify, and regulate these emotions, making them easier to bear.

Alliances and friendships shift around during a divorce, and finding your "tribe" during this tumultuous time becomes imperative. Support from friends, family, and possibly a trusted professional fosters the healing process.

The nature of the breakup affects the healing process. It is one thing if a couple splits up amicably because they have grown apart over the years. It is an entirely different kind of grieving when one partner has been blindsided by an affair. Also, different personalities respond differently to loss. Regardless of the situation or the personalities involved, the intensity of loss does eventually quiet down. Even the most unbearable pain softens with time.

The Roots of Compulsive Eating

Melissa was highly motivated to eat more consciously, and after only a few months of working together, I could see a change in her demeanor. She seemed more focused and ready to talk about other personal matters. At one of our sessions, Melissa reported feeling calmer and that her crying and anger bouts were quieting down. She now wanted to explore her struggles with food and body image.

I asked her to talk about past triggers that might have fueled her compulsive eating. Melissa thought for a while and then told me about all her lonely nights growing up. Food became her reliable companion when her mother zoned out. When Andrew grew distant, she again resorted to eating for comfort. "Andrew would go to sleep and I would fill myself with ice cream, carbs, sweets, and whatever else I could find. I started hiding food because I was afraid that he might discover my secret. I think now that he probably did not want to shame me by exposing my closet binging. He must have noticed my weight gain, but he never said a word about my weight or the emptied refrigerator.

"The only thing that calms me down is eating, but that feeling never lasts. I know the eating is doing me in and yet I can't seem to get a handle on this behavior. Every time I binge, I feel disgusting and depressed. I hate having this lack of control. Most of the time I don't even enjoy the food, but I can't stop. I desperately want to learn to eat like a normal person, without the guilt and shame."

The origins of Melissa's compulsive eating dated back to her early childhood, when food replaced love. I remarked, "For years, you filled the void with food. As a kid, this was a creative way to find comfort, but clearly the overeating is no longer serving you. The eating might temporarily quiet your anxiety and numb you from painful feelings, but in the end it takes a huge toll. You need to develop the ability to fill yourself in deeper and more satisfying ways. The food will never give you what you really need. Learning to love yourself will change your relationship with food."

Melissa had been faithfully practicing breathing several times a day. For the first time ever, she intercepted a binge by breathing abdominally and taking a brisk walk. Melissa breathed deeply, repeated her affirmation, and felt the urge to eat subside. "This," she said, "felt empowering and hopefully represented a turning point." I taught Melissa to meditate, which she also began to incorporate into her day. She was building her inner strength one day at a time.

We continued to talk about Andrew and the children, but now Melissa became determined to manage her eating. I offered to teach her a technique known as "mindful eating."

For many women, eating becomes a paradoxical setup for pleasure and pain. Eating nourishes the body, brings pleasurable sensations, and can fill us with delight. Yet it can also lead to feelings of shame and guilt for women who eat to anesthetize themselves to pain and disappointment. Triggers for compulsive eating are the same as for other addictions. The acronym H.A.L.T. is one way to remember the most salient triggers: being Hungry, Angry, Lonely, or Tired. When ignored or left unaddressed, any of these states can lead to a compulsive eating episode.

Strategy to Decrease Compulsive Eating

- Consider whether this compulsive behavior serves you or interferes with your happiness and relationships with others.

- Set a clear intention to diminish this self-defeating behavior.

- Keep a journal to track your progress. If you can track it, you can change it.

- Notice the interplay between triggers, emotions, and compulsive eating.

- Manage stress and anxiety and heighten awareness of eating behavior with mindfulness practices.

- Exercise regularly. Brisk walking or any workout routine will reduce cravings, lift your spirits, decrease stress, and improve health.

- Stop dieting! Focus on eating three nutritious meals and healthy snacks each day.

- Plan meals and stick to a schedule. Skipping meals leads to compulsive eating.

- Healthy eating is about good choices and portion control.

- Keep junk food and "binge material" out of the house.

- Get plenty of sleep and rest. Being tired is a powerful trigger.

- Find support, especially when feeling vulnerable or lonely.

- Visualize yourself having the life you desire. Use affirmations like "I can do this!"

- Take steps every day to achieve your goals.

- When you slip, forgive yourself for the lapse and swiftly get back on the path. This is all part of the healing process.

Unlike other forms of addiction, eating is essential to survival. Complicating matters, women often regard food as the culprit responsible for making them fat. Women judge themselves harshly, if not cruelly, for the way they look and food becomes the identified enemy of the idealized body. The tension that so many women experience around food and body image often runs deep and can perpetuate a loss of control around eating. Resist the notion of perfection; otherwise, you are doomed to fail. Instead, embrace the notion of "good enough" about your body and the foods you choose. Learning to accept your imperfect self will help to decrease stress and the drive to eat compulsively.

Mindful Eating

Mindful eating means deliberately paying attention to the experience of eating and drinking using all senses—without judgment. It involves the awareness of colors, textures, smells, sounds, temperature, and the arrangement of food—before, during, and after eating. Mindful eating makes the experience of ingesting conscious and strengthens concentration, sensory clarity, and inner calm. The goal is to notice what is happening in the mind and body without engaging in outside influences. When distractions come, bring your attention back, with kindness and compassion, to the focus of eating.

Often people do not like this exercise at first because it can heighten unpleasant feelings. The object is to observe moods, thoughts, and emotions with acceptance regardless of what comes to the surface. With practice, it is possible to regain our natural birthright, which is to eat with the ease and pleasure that most of us experienced in childhood.

I encouraged Melissa to practice mindful eating—ideally, alone and in silence for the first few times. I suggested she "designate one meal a week when you can practice this. If you feel the impulse to turn on the television or computer, or even to open a book, acknowledge this urge and return your attention to the eating. This takes practice, because the old habit of eating without conscious awareness is difficult to change. Making small, incremental changes like introducing one "mindful meal" a week will create a foundation. Over time, this practice will heighten your awareness and help you change your relationship with food to one that is more deeply gratifying and based in pleasure, rather than the suppression of feelings.

"Eventually, you will be able to integrate aspects of this practice into social settings. However, right now a more concentrated practice will help you internalize a deeper awareness of your relationship with food. The goal is to reclaim a sense of joy around eating, before you began to feel self-conscious and guilty about your body and the foods that you ate.

"When you sit down to your meal, notice the thoughts and feelings that enter your mind and body as you eat. Pay attention to the food you choose to eat and when you are eating out of loneliness or sadness versus hunger and pleasure. Learn to identify when you feel nourished and nurtured as opposed to stuffed and uncomfortable. As you eat, remind yourself to breathe. With practice, you will develop a more positive connection to food, your body image, and the pleasurable experience of eating."

This was a pivotal time for Melissa to begin thinking about her self-care. Creating the space in her life for conscious eating and other mindfulness practices would empower her and help cultivate her ability to make better choices.

Not surprisingly, Melissa lapsed into occasional binges and self-criticism, but she also experienced successes. Each day presented Melissa with a fresh canvas, and she now knew she had the power to create her own reality. She knew that if it was possible to get through a day eating mindfully, it was possible for her to get through two consecutive days. Her goal was to keep expanding her ability to eat in ways that supported her physically and emotionally.

Mindful Eating Strategy

- Determine whether or not you are hungry before eating.

- Do not wait until you are "starving" to eat.

- Keep a variety of healthy foods available at home and work.

- Prepare an array of foods that appeal to the senses and satisfy hunger.

- Set the table in an appealing manner.

- Sit down at the table in a comfortable position.

- Keep distractions to a minimum.

- Take a few deep breaths to relax your mind and body.

- Appreciate the food before you and what it took to get it from farm to table.

- Savor the aromas, colors, textures, and tastes as you eat.

- Put implements down between bites.

- Chew patiently and continue to pay attention to your senses as you eat.

- Put your napkin on your plate or leave the table when you are done eating.

- Notice how you feel when you are finished eating.

Melissa began to integrate the breathing, meditation, affirmations, and eating strategies into her daily routine. She developed her own system in which she practiced meditation in the morning, breathing and affirmations throughout the day, and aspects of the mindful eating at each meal, and before sleep she would use constructive rest to initiate relaxation. Once a week, she chose to practice mindful eating alone and in silence.

The binging at night persisted, so there was still work to be done, but the mindless grazing throughout the day quieted down considerably. Rather than rushing to anesthetize her emotions, Melissa now had tools to help her better tolerate her feelings, and they continued to become more internalized. I knew that once she could harness her compulsive eating behavior, her self-confidence would soar.

Thoughts About Shame and Body Image

Often combined with compulsive eating are powerful feelings of shame, poor body image, and self-disgust. Successful management of compulsive eating involves learning to recognize negative emotions and perceptions about one's body, and to replace them with more compassionate, positive responses. Mindfulness practices and reframing negative thoughts empower one to make better choices when the impulse to act compulsively shows itself.

Shame is the painful feeling caused by a person's belief that something they did was foolish or wrong—even if at the time the behavior feels beyond their control. "Healthy shame" guides us to learn, grow, and make better choices. For example, after a binge, one might feel shame and then be guided back to healthier eating. "Toxic shame" is not about a misguided decision. It is the feeling that "I" am misguided, unworthy, and unlovable. Toxic shame usually stems from early traumatic experiences or critical messages from our parents or caretakers. This powerfully disturbing feeling runs deep to the core. Overcoming toxic shame means first learning to tolerate this painful affect and then building inner resources and strengths to feel worthy and lovable.

Melissa's experience of shame dated back to her early feelings about her body, her alcoholic mother, her compulsive eating, and now the rupture in her marriage. She needed to bear these painful, deep-rooted feelings. Melissa had to learn self-kindness and compassion, and summon the courage to face her demons. Mindfulness practices and our therapeutic dialogue were helping her make these core changes. At least once a day she practiced some form of relaxation, as well as reframing her thoughts to create a positive perspective so that she could gain greater control over the old negative thoughts about her body and her compulsive eating behaviors.

Melissa's mindfulness practices became more ingrained. Her eating became less frantic and more pleasurable. She ramped up her exercise regimen and alternated between daily walks and swims. Even short walks in the fresh air left her feeling more energetic, and swimming left her feeling light and buoyant. When the cold weather came, Melissa joined a local swim club and began taking yoga classes with a couple of girlfriends. Her sense of humor started to return, and she felt better about her body than ever before. She created the space to think about her childhood and her marriage with more understanding and empathy.

Strategy for Building a Positive Body Image

- Begin the day with a few deep breaths and a positive affirmation.

- Observe how you feel about your body at different times of the day.

- Treat your body with respect and compassion.

- Participate in a regular exercise routine that builds strength, flexibility, and endurance.

- Exercise with a friend when you can; this makes working out more fun and less arduous.

- Stand, sit, and move in good posture. You will feel better physically and emotionally.

- Accept your genetics and learn to appreciate your natural body type.

- Replace or overshadow negative self-talk with breath work and affirmations.

- Focus on your unique gifts and talents that have nothing to do with appearance.

- Surround yourself with loving and supportive members of your "tribe."

Mindfulness Practices to Ease Anxiety

Melissa desperately wanted to move on with her life, although feelings of anxiety would still catch her off guard. She and Andrew struggled to come to terms with financial matters, family traditions, friendships, and lifestyle, especially as they pertained to the children. Melissa worried that the greatest fallout from the divorce would be on Daniel and Jessica. In both subtle and dramatic ways, the children showed their anger and sadness. That hurt Melissa most and reminded her of her own early fears of being abandoned.

"I've always felt anxious about one thing or another. I think it began when I was a little girl and my mother went 'missing' in the evenings. I felt anxious about eating and feeling fat, about Andrew and his unstable work life, about spending money and depending on our families for handouts, about being pregnant and having children, and about Andrew withdrawing from me. The only time I didn't feel anxious was when I first married Andrew. Now I feel anxious about getting divorced, about the children, and about being a single parent. The fear of the unknown terrifies me."

Her face flushed a deep pink. She fought back the tears. "I've been lonely and afraid most of my life. As a kid, it felt like no one would be there for me, and I was right. I believed I was neither good enough nor lovable. I prayed I could count on Andrew, but that turned out to be a fantasy." Melissa's experience was that her needs had not been met by her parents or in her marriage to Andrew. It was now up to her to take care of herself.

"Anxiety is about taking flight from painful emotions," I reminded Melissa. "Getting beyond the dread means having the courage to allow these feelings to surface and find release. You have everything you need to emerge from this divorce and lead a good life. New doors will open for you in time. For now, you need to persevere, breathe, and let the feelings come. They will quiet down in time and you will survive. Keep up your mindfulness practices and you will thrive in all kinds of surprising ways." The intensity of Melissa's emotions was bound to increase, but then, eventually, subside. I explained that anxiety is often the flip side of excitement. Although she feared this loss, she also needed to consider the potential opportunities that lay before her.

The mindfulness strategies she practiced helped Melissa to reflect on her inner world and live more in the moment. After her mini-meditations and breath work, she added a new affirmation: "I love myself unconditionally." She repeated this to herself throughout the day. Melissa was learning to love herself, rather than hoping for someone to come along and save her. She became better able to bear her emotional world, including her longstanding feelings of shame and loneliness. Melissa never imagined she could tolerate these emotions without resorting to compulsive eating.

She began keeping a journal as another tool to better understand her inner world. Writing became a critical mode of self-expression, helping her to identify and tease out complex feelings. She wrote about those lonely nights when she felt abandoned by her mother and identified the anger and grief she felt about her marriage coming undone. Melissa knew now that the only way to overcome her pain and anxiety was to be willing to feel its ferocity and trust that it would eventually quiet.

Forgiveness and Moving On

Something good was happening for Melissa. I could see a transformation occurring before my eyes. I suggested that we go a step further. "Perhaps it is time for you to forgive yourself, Andrew, and your parents for all the mistakes and disappointments."

"How can I forgive when I still feel so much anger?" she responded.

"It's challenging, but it is possible."

Learning to forgive is a skill you can cultivate. It is one of the essential keys to personal freedom and empowerment. Forgiveness does not excuse neglect or harmful actions, but it allows you to free up energy to focus on the positive aspects of your life. Developing the capacity to forgive ultimately brings inner peace.

I told Melissa, "Keep in mind that you and Andrew did the best that you could. You both had complicated pasts and hung in together all these years and created a life for yourselves and your children. Jessica and Daniel are doing well, which means you both made many good decisions. You may always carry certain regrets, but they need not define you. You are a wonderful mother, a creative, loving woman with so much to offer. Letting go of your anger and resentments will liberate you and allow you to venture freely into the next phase of your life. Forgiveness is tough to learn but worth the effort because it will help you to release your anger, better manage your eating behaviors, and improve your overall health. Using your journal as you navigate through this process will be a great companion and guide.

Ho'oponopono

There was another method I wanted to teach Melissa: the ancient Hawaiian practice of reconciliation and forgiveness known as "ho'oponopono." In this tradition, it is believed that if one remains angry, unforgiving, and isolated for long periods of time, then illness will follow. The essence of this teaching is that we are all connected and that we are all responsible for each other. Therefore, by repairing our relationships, we heal ourselves, and we heal the world.

The practice of ho'oponopono involves repentance, forgiveness, gratitude, and love. When we open our hearts to the place within another person or within ourselves that needs healing, we repeat the phrases "I am sorry," "Please forgive me," "Thank you," and "I love you." It is believed that the heartfelt expression of these four statements builds an internal sense of healing, health, and harmony. There are no documented studies that research the tradition of ho'oponopono, although it is known that being able to repent, forgive, show gratitude, and love all foster the experience of well-being.

I suggested to Melissa that she practice saying this mantra during or following one of her meditation sessions. As strange as this seemed to her initially, the meaning behind the expressions resonated with Melissa. She repeated the sound of ho'oponopono until it rolled off her tongue and felt like a word of her own. She spoke the phrases "I am sorry," "Please forgive me," "Thank you," and "I love you." This practice helped her, especially when she found herself feeling disconnected or beginning to assign blame to others.

Forgiveness Strategy

- Keep a journal to track your progress.

- Create a list of past or present events that make you feel angry, hurt, or disappointed.

- Start off by writing down more minor injustices or violations and build up to more significant ones.

- Sit comfortably in a seated position and take a few breaths, relaxing your mind and body.

- Take the least significant injustice and pair it with deep breathing until the misdeed feels less charged.

- Move down the list so that the deep breathing, visualization, and a feeling of letting go accompany each offense. Give yourself ample time to diffuse each of these past hurts. Certain painful memories may take repeated sessions.

- Practice this strategy once or twice daily for five to ten minutes to strengthen your ability to forgive, let go, and move forward.

Melissa and I continued these conversations over the next few weeks. Sometimes tears would flow, anger would surface, or a host of other emotions would emerge as we talked. She practiced forgiveness along with the other mindfulness strategies, and over time, the anger quieted and the compassion for herself, Andrew, and her parents grew.

After one of our sessions, she smiled, looked deeply into my eyes, and said, "I understand. I'm feeling something shift. It's definitely a process, but I feel my mind and body opening up to these new sensations. It's like my heart is expanding and it's not about what Andrew or my parents did or didn't do. It's about loving myself and feeling worthwhile." Melissa came to accept that at the time, she and Andrew had done the best they could. She knew there was no going back, but now felt better equipped to move forward and to discuss the children, finances, and logistics with Andrew. The next step was for Melissa to visualize what she wanted these next years to look like. I encouraged her to focus her attention on fulfilling her deepest dreams and goals for the future.

Seeking Support During the Divorce Process

Initially, Melissa had been in hiding, keeping her misery to herself. Some of Melissa's friends fell by the wayside, as happens during the divorce process. Certain friends felt like they had to choose sides while others had conflicted feelings about their own marriages and elected to keep a distance, fearing that divorce might be contagious. Once she became clear about which of her friends could offer reliable support, she began reaching out, at first reluctantly and then with enthusiasm.

Melissa reached out to her girlfriends, especially the ones she knew understood. Spending time with her friends became a great source of healing and joy. Her posse rallied around her, each one bringing unique gifts. Some friends made her laugh, some cried with her, some helped her with concrete tasks, while others whisked her away for lunch or coffee. Still others came together to help her brainstorm ways to become financially independent.

Melissa's friends stood by her over the many months of this transition. She felt buoyed by their love and support. As she embraced the present along with what she needed to do going forward, her self-esteem grew. Melissa began to let go of her past life and felt like she was unearthing her authentic self—for the first time ever. The emotional roller-coaster ride was part of the process. With her mindfulness training, Melissa's self-awareness and ability to tolerate intense feelings expanded greatly. She was coming to know that she could handle whatever life brought.

Simplifying and Building a New Life

Melissa downsized to a modest apartment in the city. She gave away furniture, outdated and ill-fitting clothing, and all the "stuff" she had accumulated over the years. Melissa felt freer as she lightened her load. She sold some things and donated others to a women's shelter. Her little apartment seemed spacious now that she had opted for greater sparseness in her life.

Over the months, Melissa continued to simplify her life, making deliberate decisions that supported her new path. As part of her decision-making process she would ask herself, "Will this make me happy?" "Will this contribute to my well-being?" She practiced saying "no" when she felt overextended or needed space. Most importantly, Melissa decided to spend time *only* with people she loved and who lifted her spirits.

She incorporated her mindfulness training into a one-hour consolidated session in which she did abdominal breathing and a ten-minute meditation, followed by her affirmation du jour. As part of her routine, Melissa also walked briskly for about twenty minutes, and the tone for her day was set. Nightly, she wrote in her journal and then carried it around with her just in case she felt moved to write. Whenever Melissa became frustrated or had the urge to eat compulsively, she would take some breaths and collect herself. Then she would write down whatever came to mind, and take stock of her thoughts and emotions. She understood that deep down she craved love and connection more than anything. On rare occasions Melissa lapsed into compulsive eating, but these episodes were short-lived. As she learned how to forgive herself for her imperfections, Melissa became better able to do so with others.

Next Steps

Shortly after moving into her apartment, Melissa launched her own web-design business. She had dreamed about building such a business for years, and now with support, renewed energy, and focus, Melissa was ready to channel her creative energies. She built a website, initiated a marketing campaign, and began networking in her community and beyond. In a matter of months, she had established a solid client base and become a known entity.

Melissa was turning forty, and her son, Daniel, was leaving for college in the fall. She had remained committed to her children as they went through their own grieving process regarding the divorce. Seeing their sadness hurt the most, but she could see that they were emerging from the darkest phase. Daniel was ready for his next move, and Melissa would be there to support him each step of the way. She was grateful to have Jessica to herself these next couple of years before her launch.

Melissa had managed to change her eating habits, which had enabled her to shed much of her extra weight. She made mindful decisions about how she ate and rediscovered the pleasure of eating. With the walking, swimming, and occasional yoga classes, Melissa felt stronger, sexier, and more invigorated. In time she began to date. Excited and scared, Melissa started to feel ready to meet men, perhaps even find a new partner.

Over time, the pain of her childhood and failed marriage quieted and Melissa became excited about the potential in the years ahead. She now regarded her failed marriage as the necessary push needed to resolve a lifelong history of unhealthy thoughts and behaviors. Six months into the dating scene, Melissa met a man she greatly enjoyed, and she decided to move slowly. She felt optimistic as she eased her way back to intimacy, knowing and feeling for the first time in her life that she no longer needed a man to save her. Melissa had courageously delved deep inside and worked hard to access her inner strength. There was no going back.

CHAPTER SIX

A Life-Threatening Diagnosis

Sophie

Sophie's chin-length, platinum hair framed her tanned complexion and piercing steel-blue eyes. Dressed in bright white tennis shoes and a dark-gray warm-up suit, she was an athletic forty-six-year-old who looked like she'd come straight off the court. Sophie, her husband Michael, and their two young children, Sam, nine, and Abigail, seven, lived in town.

Sophie came in for an initial consultation because she had been feeling inordinate sadness and anxiety ever since her identical twin sister, Laurie, was diagnosed with breast cancer. Crying spells had become routine, and Sophie began isolating herself from friends. Feelings of dread pervaded her everyday life, and she felt unmotivated to perform her regular responsibilities. In a monotone voice, she explained, "Laurie's diagnosis came as a total shock. Cancer does not run in our family. The threat of potentially losing my sister is more than I can handle, and I've been completely preoccupied with my own mortality. Both my parents died in recent years, and I can't bear another loss.

"I came from such a loving, tight-knit family, and now everything seems to be falling apart." Sophie needed to share her story. The threat of losing Laurie had stirred powerful and unresolved feelings regarding the loss of her parents, and now terror struck as she considered the possibility of losing her sister. My goal was to help Sophie develop tools to manage her immobilizing fear, process her grief, and gain perspective on the losses that threatened her well-being.

When I asked Sophie to share some information about her background, she began by telling me, "I was a practicing nurse for years and know a great deal about disease and illness, which is why I am so worried about Laurie. Even though they caught her cancer early, I know all the possible complications."

I asked her why she left her nursing career. She said, "My son Sam was born with a heart defect and needed surgery when he was only three months old. Thankfully, he is healthy now. It was then that I took a leave from my career to devote myself to his care. A couple of years later Abigail was born, and I just wanted to be with my children. I began volunteering at a local hospice to satisfy my passion for my work, and I've been there ever since. I needed to feel like I was using my skills and making a difference, but I also wanted the flexibility to be available to my family. Lately, however, there has been absolutely no time for anything other than focusing on my sister. I need to do whatever I can to help."

I asked if Laurie had a family of her own, which she did. Sophie insisted that although her sister had a supportive husband and good friends, she needed to be there for Laurie whenever possible.

The Family

"Laurie has such a warrior spirit," said Sophie. "She's an incredible mother. Her composure and positive attitude, especially around her daughters, are her way of protecting them from unnecessary worry. I just can't stop my thoughts from going to the darkest places.

"I've been trekking back and forth to Laurie's in New York every weekend for the last few months, and I'm exhausted and angry that this is happening to my sister. It's beyond unfair that someone so good could be stricken like this, out of nowhere. She doesn't smoke or drink; she eats well and takes good care of herself. I just don't understand.

"It makes matters worse that both of our parents are gone, so it's just the two of us now. Our mother died suddenly of a heart attack ten years ago, and then our father died two years ago in the same shocking way. Now, caring for my own children and running back and forth to New

York every week is so exhausting. I feel like I have nothing left to give, but I have to carry on. I still haven't gotten over the loss of my mother, let alone my dad. Sometimes I feel like I can't breathe when I think about them being gone."

"Tell me more about them," I urged.

Sophie's eyes filled and her body sank into the couch. "My mother's death was so sudden and unexpected. There was no preparation. No apparent illness. She was alive one minute and gone the next. My mother was on one of her early Sunday morning walks, and just before returning home, she evidently stopped and sat down on a neighbor's lawn. A couple of women passing by recognized her and checked to see if she was okay. My mother responded that she had suddenly become tired and just needed to rest. She collapsed, and the women immediately called 911 and my father, who had been waiting for her at home. He frantically ran down the block and found my mother lying there. My father held her in his arms and commanded her to wake up, crying in total despair. When the ambulance arrived, they tried resuscitating her, but it was too late. She was pronounced dead right there in front of my father. He fell apart. In the end the medics had to restrain him so that they could take her away.

I don't know too many details after that, even to this day. She was only seventy and so full of life, always planning the next trip, the next adventure. Her family was her world. Before the funeral I opened the casket, just to check, because I simply could not wrap my head around my mother really being gone. It didn't look like her. I remember thinking the whole thing was a terrible mistake. I could not see my vital mother in that rigid, lifeless body. Laurie peeled me away from the casket and begged me to keep it together, which I somehow managed to do. Laurie was always more stoic, but my mother's death somehow changed us forever. Suddenly, everything about our lives became less permanent and more precarious.

"For months, I cried spontaneously, in the middle of the most mundane activities—cleaning, cooking, exercising, going to my kids' school events, and, of course, on every holiday or special occasion. Every day I miss her. We were blessed to have grown up with a mother capable of such unconditional love. To this day, I sometimes forget that she's gone. I pick up the phone and this sickening feeling comes over me, and

I remember. In my head, I talk to her about whatever is going on in my life, especially regarding the children, my marriage, and now Laurie.

"About a year after my mother died, my father started dating. It was too weird for me to think about, but he needed to talk to Laurie and me about the women in his life and how to handle all kinds of situations. My mother's death was traumatic for him, but he was determined not to roll over and die. It was painful talking to my father about dating other women, but I knew he needed to move on for his own sake.

"About six months into dating, he met a woman, Helen, who seemed to capture his attention. They courted for several months. She was a comfortable companion and liked to golf, play cards, and take long cruises. They were good for each other. My father moved to the posh Florida community where she already lived and they quickly built a life together, although they never married. Father dropped most of the friends that he and our mother shared, as they reminded him too much of his old life. He seemed happy enough, although I don't think he ever got over the loss of my mother.

"Laurie's and my relationship with Helen revolved solely around our father. We remained cordial and kept a healthy distance. Father needed space to navigate through this time of life his own way. We visited periodically and celebrated certain holidays together. About seven years into their relationship, I got the call that my father had had a massive heart attack and died before he ever reached the hospital. Once again, there was no warning or preparation. He was alive one minute and gone the next, just like my mother. It was devastating. It was good he did not suffer, but again Laurie and I were left reeling."

Sophie's face flushed, but she kept her emotions in check. I reflected, "You've had considerable loss over the past few years. It's frightening and everything feels so out of control when you lose people in your life that you love so profoundly."

She came from a family where they took care of one another, celebrating each other's joys and successes and rallying around each other in times of need. Sophie and Laurie often spoke several times a day, to problem-solve, to commiserate, to connect. Being close to her sister seemed more important now than ever.

Sophie sat in silence, lost in thought.

"I'm sorry for your losses," I offered. "I can understand how painful this had to be for you and your sister."

Sophie burst into tears. "I can't handle the thought of losing Laurie. She is all I have left of my family. We share everything with each other. She is so vibrant and nurturing. There is absolutely no justice in this. Her diagnosis feels like the last straw. I can't sleep. I can't think clearly. Losing my parents was awful, but at least that's the natural course of things. Laurie is forty-five, with a great family and a full life in front of her. I can't take any more loss. She is all the family I have left."

I reminded Sophie that her sister was not dying, that I knew she was scared, but she needed to keep this in perspective. The advances regarding breast cancer treatment have been nothing short of remarkable. I asked how Laurie was managing with her treatments.

"Laurie is strong. She's taking this as well as anyone can, but it's been such a blow. For some reason, she won't talk to me about the physical stuff she's going through. I'm sure she's thinking about her mortality. She has a small group of friends, and I think she is sharing with them because she's afraid I'll get too emotional. Laurie has always been fiercely protective of the people closest to her. She relies on her husband, Steven, her few friends, and me in different ways. She never permits herself to become a burden.

"The great news is that the doctor found cancer in only a single node in her breast. She is going every other week for treatment and, thankfully, is tolerating all the drugs and interventions well. Her doctor says that her case is straightforward and that Laurie should be fine. Still, I'm anxious during the day and occasionally have nightmares. I just want this to be behind us."

Sorting Out Past Loss

Sophie was struggling with the loss of her mother and father, who both suffered premature deaths. She did not know how to manage the overwhelming emotions she felt about her sister's cancer diagnosis. In the past when life became challenging, Sophie had always relied on her mother, her father, or Laurie. She came to therapy, as these options were not available to her now. Sophie desperately needed to talk about her inner world and to learn how to bear her anxiety and fear regarding Laurie's prognosis. At our first session I taught her abdominal breathing in the constructive-rest position. I knew this would help her find a greater sense of ease so that she could better regulate her emotions.

In the sessions that followed, we talked about Sophie's family of origin and the family she created with Michael. We talked about how she might be better able to care for herself. Caring for herself had somehow gotten lost during the years spent mourning the loss of her parents and now the stress around Laurie's diagnosis. Our conversations, along with the focus on abdominal breathing during the day and the constructive rest at night, were helping Sophie to find some semblance of control.

Self-Care

At one of our next sessions, I offered, "It sounds like Laurie is in good hands and is tolerating the treatment well. She has good support, her doctor is optimistic, and she is surrounded by so much love. Perhaps this is a good time for you to take some time for yourself—to be with your family, to exercise, to rest, maybe even to have some fun. Perhaps it might even be okay for you to occasionally visit with Laurie by Skype or iChat so that you can free up some time for your needs. I don't think this is selfish; quite the contrary: I believe it is self-preservative. My guess is that you will be better able to manage your anxiety and be more available to Laurie and your own family if you keep yourself strong and nourished."

Sophie clearly wanted guidance as she navigated through the process of self-care. I taught her how to meditate. I recited the cues, and she carefully followed my instructions. "Relax your eyes closed as you sit comfortably on the couch. Watch the rise and fall of your breath, repeating the word *in* to yourself as you breathe in, and *out* to yourself as you breathe out. When thoughts come to mind, observe where your mind goes. No judgment—just observation. Then gently and compassionately bring your attention back to the breath—breathing *in* and breathing *out*." We did this for about ten minutes, and Sophie began to feel calmer and more focused on the present. I told her that this technique reduces fatigue, pain, fear, anxiety, high blood pressure, stress, and shortness of breath—all while fostering insight, feelings of calm, and inner peace. I knew Sophie would benefit from meditation and suggested that she teach it to her sister as well. Perhaps they could even practice together during their visits.

Abdominal breathing came easily for Sophie and she practiced it periodically throughout the day, and specifically whenever anxious thoughts came to mind. I explained that learning to manage her anxiety during the day would eventually improve her sleep and allow her nightmares to subside.

In spite of her initially positive experience in my office, Sophie had a tougher time practicing seated meditation. She felt antsy and clearly preferred being in action mode. I suggested that walking mindfully outside in the fresh air would be a good alternative form of meditation for her.

Mindful Walking

Mindful walking, or walking meditation, combines the basic principles of the breath-focused attention of a seated meditation with rhythmic walking. I explained to Sophie, "Rather than repeating the words *in* and *out,* think about the words *heel, toe* as you move through each step. When your mind wanders, gently bring your attention back to this focus. Again, no judgments—just observations."

When a person is anxious or fearful, a seated meditation can sometimes feel antithetical to what the body needs to be doing energetically. It often feels good to harness anxious feelings and restlessness with a mindful walk. The benefits of mindful walking are quite similar to those of traditional meditation. They include a decrease in heart rate and blood pressure, enhanced feelings of well-being, improved quality of sleep, better overall stress management, and increased resiliency.

Mindful Walking Strategy

- Choose a place where you can walk comfortably and safely, preferably in nature.

- Remain aware of your breath and the space around you.

- Observe feelings and sensations.

- Feel your feet as they contact the ground.

- Repeat the words *heel, toe* as you focus on each step.

- When your mind wanders from this focus, gently bring your attention back.

- Observe whatever thoughts come to mind, without judgment.

- Be patient. This skill is easy to learn, but takes practice to master.

- Walk for ten to twenty minutes or more.

The Annual Mammogram

For Sophie, the mindful walking enabled her to channel her energy, develop greater introspection, and get fresh air and exercise. The following week she was scheduled for her own annual mammogram. As in past years, she received a callback for additional films due to the density of her breasts. Although this was not new to her, this time the callback felt scarier than usual. At Sophie's next therapy appointment, she told me, "The radiologist found a calcification in one of my breasts that had changed since last year. He assured me that most calcifications are insignificant and that I have nothing to worry about, but nevertheless he ordered a routine needle biopsy. When I told him about my sister, he listened but didn't seem particularly concerned. He assured me that everything was protocol. 'Go home and relax and we'll continue the conversation when we have the data.'"

Sophie continued, "I went home. The sun was shining and I must have walked for two hours. I kept reminding myself to breathe. I just walked in the sunshine, breathing deeply and trying to be present without jumping to conclusions. There is about a two-week wait to get the biopsy results. My sister is in the middle of radiation treatments and seems to be doing fine, and I'm freaking out not being able to share this with her. Michael is being wonderful and was with me this time for the mammogram and biopsy, but I don't want the kids to know what I'm going through. They've already seen too much with my parents and Laurie."

Sophie looked exhausted and scared. I asked her if she had been sleeping.

"I can't sleep and I'm not thinking straight. I'm putting up this façade for Laurie, which is such a drain. I miss her support. The walks continue to help, but only for a short while."

I said to Sophie, "Being secretive about your diagnosis keeps you lonely and can be a terrible burden. Maybe you can reconsider letting Laurie know what's going on. She sounds like a strong woman and can probably handle hearing this information. My guess is that Laurie could be a source of comfort to you." Sophie would not yield; she had to protect her sister.

I asserted, "If you can't sleep, at least allow your body to rest. Practice abdominal breathing in the constructive-rest position in bed. If that doesn't work, some sort of sleep medication could be a temporary solution. You'll be better equipped to handle the stress and worry if you get some rest.

A few days later, we met again. Sophie told me she had been walking at least once a day and was getting into the constructive-rest position whenever she needed to relax. She had also started taking prescribed medication, as needed, for sleep. However, her mind still raced and took her to terrifying places. Sophie wanted to talk to Laurie but decided to wait until she got the biopsy results.

We continued to talk about Sophie's fears and associations. She came to see me the morning of the day she was to get her results. It was Friday. Michael planned to come home early to be with Sophie when the news came. Her body trembled as she spoke: "I feel out of control and cannot bear what this is doing to me. I'm living in terror. It's like an out-of-body experience, only it's me and my body!" We planned to speak later that evening.

Sophie called, as promised. "The call from the doctor came hours later than expected and I somehow knew before I picked up the phone that it was bad news. He told me in a calm, straightforward manner that the biopsy showed cancer cells and I needed to meet with a breast surgeon first thing Monday morning. How could this be happening? I don't understand. I have to tell my family because I can't handle this without them."

The next morning, we met. With puffy eyes and hunched shoulders, she whispered: "I'm not as brave as Laurie. I need to have her on board." Tears streamed down her cheeks. Finally she said, "I think limbo is the worst hell of all." We spent the remainder of the session in near silence. I encouraged her to lie down on the couch, close her eyes, and breathe. She slept for a while, and I sat with her until she was ready to leave.

The news got worse. Unlike Laurie's tumor, Sophie's cancer was detected in her lymph nodes. Of the eleven nodes tested, nine were positive, indicating Stage III breast cancer. Instead of trips to support her sister, Sophie would need to conserve her energy to get through the next few months of treatments. She needed all the additional support she could rally, including meeting regularly with me.

Following her surgery, I met with her in the hospital. She looked weak but somehow more rested. Her sallow complexion gave way to a pinkish glow. She said, "I feel so blessed to have my family. Laurie, Michael, and the kids were with me, along with the surgeon, when I opened my eyes after surgery. The next step is to make sure the cancer is completely contained, but I feel hopeful. The surgeon said all the margins looked clean." Something felt different about Sophie. Instead of sheer terror, she seemed grateful to be alive.

A Breast Cancer Diagnosis

A breast cancer diagnosis can profoundly challenge a woman's physical, psychological, social, and spiritual well-being. Many women, often in the prime of life, feel blindsided and betrayed by their own bodies when they receive this diagnosis. Facing the prospect of one's own mortality or that of a loved one, even when survival rates are high, can be terrifying. However, there are ways to carry on, grow, and even thrive in the face of this diagnosis and its associated treatments.

Common, normal emotional responses following diagnosis include denial, anxiety, helplessness, anger, guilt, despair, and fear. For some women, once the initial turmoil and grief dissipate, serious psychological issues may develop. Findings from the Columbia University Medical Center in 2013 revealed that nearly one in four breast cancer patients have symptoms of post-traumatic stress disorder (PTSD) shortly after they receive their diagnosis, and this risk is highest among women of color.[13] PTSD or not, this is an acutely stressful period in a woman's life. This is why a strong support system of family, friends, and healthcare providers is so important during this time.

For many people, "the big C" conjures up images of suffering and death. According to the American Cancer Society, about one out of every eight women, or 12 percent, will be diagnosed with breast cancer during their lifetime.[14] Thankfully, dying from breast cancer is far less common, about one in thirty-six women. Treatment and early detection have continued to improve, and death rates have steadily declined since 1989. At the time of publishing, there are over 2.9 million breast cancer survivors in the United States.[15] Even though heart disease is the leading cause of death among women, the fear of developing breast cancer is greater.

A breast cancer diagnosis and the associated treatment options become a wake-up call to build a more conscious life. Contending with this diagnosis means being proactive by getting an education about treatment protocols. It involves developing the ability to observe, express, and tolerate terrifying emotions and maintaining a rock-solid support system. During this critical time, it is important to gather or sometimes

[13] http://neurosciencenews.com/ptsd-breast-cancer-newly-diagnosed/ (accessed January 9, 2017).

[14] http://www.breastcancer.org/symptoms/understand_bc/statistics (accessed January 10, 2017).

[15] http://www.cancer.org/cancer/breastcancer/detailedguide/breast-cancer-key-statistics (accessed January 10, 2017).

reinvent your "posse," choosing friends, family, and support groups that are fully committed to helping foster the healing process.

Creating a life of meaning and quality under the duress of the unknown is the challenge. Yet there are strategies that can be implemented to lower stress and anxiety, improve sleep and relaxation, and develop a more positive mind-set. Authentic connection with others or even writing in a journal allows one to clarify and release inner angst. Many women keep a blog as they go through their journey with breast cancer treatment and recovery. While this requires a willingness to be vulnerable and tolerate exposure, blogging can open the door for personal expression and greater connection.

Mindfulness practices like meditation, abdominal breathing, visualization, and self-hypnosis are powerful ways to reduce stress and develop a more optimistic perspective. Light exercise like walking, gentle yoga, Tai Chi, and swimming can have a deeply calming effect on the mind and body.

For many women, surviving cancer can lead to a more conscious life. Frequently, during the treatment and healing process, women learn to take charge of their lives as never before. Life is not quite the same after one receives a breast cancer diagnosis. Women often speak of their gratitude not only for surviving this disease but also for learning to engage more deeply in their daily lives. Learning to savor the moments of each day and make time for fun and play takes on new significance. Many survivors also report developing a deep sense of purpose, to give, to serve, to make a difference in the lives of others. We cannot necessarily control the events that take place in our lives, but we can choose how we respond to these events. Sophie's charge was to gather the strength and tools to help her triumph over loss and adversity. This would be our work together over the next couple of years.

The Elements of Self-Hypnosis

Sophie needed tools and support now. I knew she would benefit from learning a self-hypnosis strategy. I found this method to be quite healing and affirming when going through difficult transitions, particularly medical interventions. This self-hypnosis technique combines relaxation with the use of visualization, sensory experiences, and affirmations. As I explained to her, "Self-hypnosis is simple to learn and can be an effective method for training the mind to think with greater courage and optimism. You already have a great attitude, and this is just another tool to build inner strength.

"For this exercise, it is important to allow yourself to see, feel, and believe that there will be a strong, positive outcome. Self-hypnosis can be practiced as often as you like. The more you 'rehearse' this method in a relaxed state of mind, the more these messages will become embedded in your brain. We will first need to establish your affirmation and then practice the visualization. Finally, both of these techniques will be merged into the self-hypnosis exercise. It will become clear once we practice together."

More About Affirmations

As we have discussed in other chapters, affirmations are simple, positive statements that ideally pass from the conscious mind to the unconscious mind. The affirmation must be believable and within the realm of possibility, though not necessarily true—yet. To work optimally, it must also evoke positive thoughts and feelings. Each affirmation needs to be personal and stated in the present tense, for example: "I feel healthy, strong, and resilient" and "I love myself unconditionally."

Affirmations repeated when the mind and body are relaxed have the most potent effect, as that is when we are most receptive to suggestions. The affirmation statement can be changed or modified as needed and can help shape thoughts and behaviors over time. I described an affirmation to Sophie as a "strong, positive message that serves as a reminder that all is well despite any lingering negative thoughts that may be lurking in the back of your mind. It is about replacing thoughts of fear with thoughts of resilience and empowerment. Most importantly, you must find an affirmation that resonates with you."

We talked about numerous possibilities and finally settled on the affirmation "Whatever happens, I know I can handle it." She wrote it down on a note and put it on her bedside table. I suggested she would feel more in control and empowered as she practiced this technique. This was a skill she could learn in minutes but would have forever.

Visualization/Imagery

Visualization or imagery is about holding a mental image or visual perception in mind. For example, you can visualize a clear blue sky, the ocean, the mountains, a meadow, a cozy bed, or a blank movie screen. To create greater feelings of relaxation, you can choose any place or object, real or imagined, with which you associate feelings of inner calm. When you close your eyes and conjure up your chosen mental image, a relaxation response eventually takes hold. With practice, the ability to conjure up positive imagery becomes stronger and more deeply embedded in the brain. Visualization itself is a relaxation technique. When it is combined with an affirmation and the involvement of the other senses, it becomes self-hypnosis.

The Countdown and Count Up Technique

Another very brief and effective relaxation technique is "the Countdown," which is exactly as its name describes. The idea is to count down from five to one, making suggestions to yourself about relaxing as you count. For example, you can say to yourself, "I am going to count down now from five to one and when I reach the number one, I will relax completely mentally and physically. *Five:* I am relaxing all the muscles of my face, especially the small muscles around my eyes and jaw. *Four:* I am relaxing my shoulders, arms, and hands. My shoulders are draping directly over my torso. *Three:* I am breathing abdominally, breathing in, breathing out, and letting go. *Two:* I can feel the full weight of my body supported by the chair as I sit comfortably. *One:* I feel a deep sense of mental and physical relaxation.

After counting down, you might choose to remain in this relaxed state for a few minutes to receive optimal benefit. To release yourself from this deep state, count up from one to five, again making suggestions and associations. The suggestions are about coming back into the present moment with a renewed state of *relaxed attentiveness*. Relaxed attentiveness is about being calm and energized at the same time, a completely compatible response.

An example of counting up might be "I am going to count up now from one to five. When I reach the number five, I will open my eyes and feel relaxed, refreshed, and revitalized, more so than before. *One:* Coming out slowly. *Two:* My breath is deep and rhythmic. *Three:* I can feel the contact my feet are making with the floor and my body is making with the chair. *Four:* I feel myself present in this room and aware of my surroundings. *Five:* Without making any fast or abrupt movements, I am gradually opening my eyes feeling relaxed, refreshed, and revitalized, more so than before. I will carry this feeling with me throughout the day."

Being relaxed and being energized are compatible responses that help optimize performance and a sense of well-being.

Countdown–Count Up Strategy

- Get into a comfortable seated position.
- Take several abdominal breaths to relax the mind and body.
- Relax from head to toe as you count down from five to one.
- Make suggestions to yourself to relax more deeply as you count down.
- When you reach number one, use the affirmation "I feel a deep sense of relaxation."
- Spend a couple of minutes settling into this feeling.
- When ready, count up from one to five.
- Make suggestions about bringing renewed vitality to the mind and body.
- When you reach number five, use the affirmation "I feel relaxed, refreshed, and revitalized—more so than before."
- Gradually, open your eyes and notice how you feel.

This technique is used in self-hypnosis and can also be practiced on its own.

Bringing It Together in Self-Hypnosis

I asked Sophie if she was ready to put all the pieces together and begin to practice self-hypnosis. She sat up tall on the couch and took some abdominal breaths and nodded. I told Sophie I would talk her through the exercise, but she would soon be able to do this on her own. She needed only a few minutes to feel the benefits of the self-hypnosis, but she could practice for longer whenever she wished.

I started with the countdown. "I am going to count down from five to one, and when we reach the number one you will relax completely mentally and physically. *Five:* Relax your eyes closed, allowing them to roll slightly upward. Relax all of your facial muscles, particularly the muscles around your eyes. Part your lips slightly to disengage your jaw and relax your tongue. *Four:* Relax your shoulders, so that they fall directly over your torso. Allow your chest and belly to open and expand. *Three:* Take a couple of deep breaths as you settle into the couch. Feel the full weight of your body being supported while you sit effortlessly. *Two:* Feel the contact your feet are making with the floor. Your feet are relaxed and fully supported. *One:* You are sitting comfortably and your mind and body are completely relaxed.

"Now think of a place where you feel comfortable and peaceful, where you have positive associations or memories." Sophie told me she loved the beach on a warm, sun-drenched, breezy day. "That's a perfect image. Take a couple of deep breaths and then in your mind's eye allow yourself to go to this beautiful place. Imagine yourself there and involve all of your senses—taste, touch, sight, sound, and smell." I gave Sophie a moment or two to delve into each of these sensations, allowing her to summon up her own imagery.

Then came the affirmation. "Release the image of the beach and repeat your affirmation, 'Whatever happens, I know I can handle it.' Imagine yourself feeling strong and empowered; involve all of your senses." I paused after a few minutes, then counted up from one to five, bringing her back into the present moment. It went something like this: "*One:* Come out slowly. *Two:* Breathe abdominally. *Three:* Visualize yourself in this room at this time. *Four:* Feel your mind and body become more awake and aware of your surroundings. *Five:* Without making any fast or abrupt movements, gradually begin opening your eyes and feel relaxed, refreshed, and revitalized, more so than before."

She gradually opened her eyes, and I detected a faint smile on her face. "I generally don't like to do stuff like that, but I really let myself go this time. It felt good. I think self-hypnosis might help when I undergo all the testing they're planning to do to make sure the cancer hasn't spread. They're going to do a set of CAT scans and bone scans later today."

"It will help," I encouraged her. "That's a perfect time to transport yourself to someplace nurturing. This exercise is available to you whenever you want a boost or to disengage. If you're finding that you're not in the mood for the visualization or self-hypnosis, you can simply practice abdominal breathing. That will help too."

Self-Hypnosis Strategy

- Find a quiet and comfortable space.
- Settle into a comfortable seated position and relax your eyes closed.
- Create an affirmation.
- Count down slowly from five to one. As you count down, relax your mind and body.
- Imagine yourself at your ideal place of relaxation.
- Involve all of your senses as you imagine yourself in this setting.
- Spend a few minutes in this deepened state; visualize and savor this experience.
- Release the image of your ideal place, and now imagine a blank screen.
- Repeat the affirmation you created earlier in this exercise.
- On this new blank screen, picture yourself enacting the affirmation.

- Involve all of your senses—taste, touch, sight, sound, and smell.

- Remain in this deepened state for several minutes.

- When you are ready, release the affirmation and gradually open your eyes.

- Count up from one to five.

- Make the suggestion that you feel relaxed, refreshed, revitalized— more so than before.

Notice how you are feeling. With practice, you will become better at each phase of this self-hypnosis strategy. Once familiar with this technique, you can practice it just about anywhere in a matter of minutes. Eventually, you will be able to tailor your self-hypnosis experience so it becomes a useful tool for helping you move toward the realization of any goal.

Sophie's eyes began to fill with tears. "Doing this exercise reminds me of my parents and how I miss them so. We used to love going to the beach together, even after my mother got sick. Those images and memories came flooding back when we practiced the visualization. It was okay, though. It felt good to revisit those special moments. I know I'll practice this because it reminds me of their love and support, which will give me courage."

Continuing Bonds

The return of a heightened feeling of loss is not a setback in the grieving process, but rather an expression of the continuing bond between parent and child. I explained this to Sophie. "Your parents are with you internally. Think about the things they would have said to you and the way they would have cared for you. Dig deep to access them and listen to the messages they would give you if they could be here with you now. Consider intentionally working them into your visualization exercises."

Sophie nodded, walked slowly to the door, and said, "Whatever happens, I can do this." Over the next couple of weeks, we met regularly as Sophie went through a multitude of tests. She continued to share stories about her parents, her marriage, her beautiful son and daughter, and Laurie. Sophie talked, laughed, and cried. At last, she received the wonderful news that her cancer had not spread. She came to her appointment looking radiant. "I'm going to be okay, and I feel it in my whole being. I feel like my mother and father are watching over me. It sounds like after chemo and radiation, I should be fine. I know there's a tough road ahead, but there is a light at the end of the tunnel."

Sophie was scheduled for four months of chemotherapy, an every-other-week regimen. The day after each chemo treatment, the nurse was to administer an injection of a medication designed to prevent Sophie's white blood cell count from dropping too low.

She missed her next appointment. I received a message from Michael telling me there were complications and Sophie had needed to be hospitalized. I tried calling her, but to no avail. After she was released from the hospital, I went to her home for our next meeting and she explained what had happened. "Several hours after I got home the evening of the first injection, I found myself writhing in pain on the bathroom floor in a puddle of sweat. Michael had gone out to get some groceries and came home to find me passed out. He rushed me to the hospital and I just remember waking up with Michael sitting nearby. He wasn't even supposed to touch me. Two nurses wearing masks and gloves were hovering over me, managing the lines and fluids going into my body.

"I received a cocktail of medicines that brought me out of the excruciating pain. I felt so disconnected from reality. The last thing I remember is seeing myself contorting on the bathroom floor, unable to control the spasms. I spent six days in an isolation ward, with nurses and doctors coming and going, all looking like something out of a science-fiction movie. They were dressed in these space suits to protect me from them, as my immune system had shut down. I was desperately ill. I must have repeated to myself a thousand times, 'Whatever happens, I can handle this.' It gave me something to focus on when I was hanging on by a thread.

"I had an allergic reaction to the medication. As a result, the chemo will take longer than expected and the post-chemo medication will be doled out less often and in much smaller doses. My body simply cannot handle the other treatment protocol."

Sophie's shallow breathing gave way to small, convulsive sobs.

"What an ordeal, Sophie. I'm so glad you're okay. It sounds like Michael was completely available and supportive."

"He's been great. When we were in the hospital, he took such exquisite care of me. No matter how tired or scared he was, he made me feel loved and safe. Laurie has also been wonderful. She calls several times a day. The wonderful news is that her treatments are finally over and her doctor says she is cancer-free. I'm so relieved."

Sophie sat silently for a bit and then closed her eyes and slept for a few minutes. When she opened her eyes, she said softly, "This is going to be harder than I thought. This was the first time I truly felt terrified. I'm a fighter, but this came on with such a vengeance. It was completely beyond my control."

"Some of this is going to be out of your control," I assured her. "Getting cancer was out of your control. This new treatment protocol will take longer, but seems like it will be less toxic to your system. The doctors now understand your body's sensitivity to the medication and will watch over you even more vigilantly." Sophie nodded limply and told me she needed to sleep.

I offered to meet her again in her home for our next appointment. She answered, "Coming to our sessions is my only reason for getting out of the house these days, besides going to the hospital. It's one of my goals to keep coming to you. I'll be there next week."

As promised, Sophie showed up for her next session, her thick blond hair cut short now, revealing small bald patches. "I'm already losing my hair. A handful came out when I was showering this morning. I know exactly what to expect and still I find it absolutely shocking. I'm not that vain a person, but this is such a blow to my ego. Nothing prepares you for looking in the mirror and seeing the puffiness, the missing patches of hair, eyebrows, and eyelashes. I know it's temporary and minor in the scheme of things, but it feels like such a violation. I have to let go of my vision of myself and remind myself what is really important. I have so much to be grateful for, and I honestly believe that ultimately I will have my health again."

She looked directly at me. Her blue eyes looked even more pensive with her closely cropped haircut. As her eyes began to well up, she asked, "What if Michael doesn't find me attractive anymore? What if he doesn't want to sleep with me and finds my body repulsive?"

"Michael loves you to the core. The cancer is making him realize, more than ever, how precious you are to him. It might be valuable for you to talk with him about your concerns. In addition, it might be helpful to practice your self-hypnosis exercise and affirmations as you go through this physical transformation."

Joining a Support Group

Sophie had a loving and supportive family and a great cadre of girlfriends who were available to her in many different and vital ways. Still, I thought it would be good for her to join a support group with other women in the throes of cancer treatment and recovery. I said, "I know you have a great support system at home, but being with a group of women who are going through what you're going through offers something that your family and friends cannot provide. I know your hospital has these groups and they're usually quite helpful, often in unexpected ways. There is no guarantee that a particular group will be a perfect fit, but generally there's something of value to be derived. Research has repeatedly shown that women who participate in these support groups have an easier recovery and sometimes a better outcome than those who do not."

"I'm such a private person that my instinct is to say 'no way,' but I think it might be a good thing for me," Sophie replied. "I don't want to burden my family and friends. There are certain things I don't want to discuss with them, but that might be good to share with other women dealing with the same issues."

The following month, Sophie joined a cancer support group that met weekly. The women ranged in age from their early twenties to late seventies. They quickly bonded and opened up about their fears, losses, and experiences. Everyone had a compelling story. Sophie loved the camaraderie of the group. Laughter and tears came with each meeting, as did new perspectives about the experience of undergoing cancer treatment. They shared with, honored, and cared for one another.

The benefits of participating in a support group during cancer treatment include:

- Connecting with others undergoing similar experiences.
- Speaking freely about thoughts, feelings, and experiences in a safe space.
- Swapping tips and advice about navigating through treatment.
- Sharing updates about treatment research, options, and outcomes.
- Diminished feelings of anxiety and stress.
- Heightened self-awareness and feelings of empowerment.

"The women are remarkable," Sophie observed. "This group brings me together with people with whom I normally would not have crossed paths, and I love these connections. It's helping me get clear on who and what's important in my life. I feel like I'm changing at a core level these days."

I asked her, "How do you feel you're changing?"

"For one thing, I've always been the caretaker in our family. All of a sudden, Michael's been thrown into that role. He's been managing me, the kids, the house, everything, and he's doing a magnificent job. I'm such a control freak. I've always needed things done a particular way. I've had to let go and allow myself to be cared for. The truth is, I am vulnerable now and need the help. I'm grateful for Michael's extraordinary kindness and capabilities. I've never seen this side of him, and I am so proud of the way he's stepped up.

"I'm also keenly aware of the many ways my friends have risen to the occasion. They have been so kind and caring. I never realized how these small acts of kindness could make such a profound difference. There are a few friends who don't know what to do or are unavailable to me because of whatever is going on in their lives. I don't want to have to educate anyone about how to behave around me. What I have noticed, though, is that spending time with certain friends feels better than with others. I am choosing to surround myself exclusively with friends I can count on to be uplifting.

"Last week, a girlfriend of mine brought me a big bag of pachysandras that she plucked from her garden and then spent the afternoon planting them around my porch. They are beginning to flourish already. Every time I see them, I feel happy and think of her loving gesture. Another girlfriend designed a schedule for various friends to bring dinner to my house each afternoon. The meals are delicious and taste like pure love. A neighbor I hardly know brought scented oils and a candle and left them at my front door along with a poem. It's such a gift to have these women in my life. As far as I'm concerned, these acts of loving kindness are really what matter most, and not just during frightening times like this."

Sophie began her next session with "Time feels so precious now and I want to savor every moment possible. While I believe I am going to emerge from this intact, it is impossible to really know the outcome. The doctors are afraid that I run the risk of infection, so I can't go out in public, anywhere. I'm tethered to my home, the hospital, and my medical appointments. This part is hard because I always loved going to my children's sporting events, parent-teacher meetings, and, of course, movies, dinners, and social events. All of that is on hold for now except for visits from friends and family.

Several months later Sophie was given the go-ahead to spend limited amounts of time in public. She shared at one of her sessions, "I won't fritter away time with anyone who doesn't understand, or for some reason is not giving me what I need. It sounds selfish, but I'm following my instincts about how to care for myself. I am also paying close attention to what feels intuitively right for me and will help me get better faster. My boundaries are stronger and more defined than ever before."

She continued coming for her weekly sessions. Sophie's breast cancer diagnosis was life-changing in multiple ways. She was inspired by her sister Laurie's bravery as she fought her own battle with the disease. Joining a support group and tapping into the loving kindness of her friends and family enhanced her well-being.

Sharing her story and practicing her mindful walking, self-hypnosis, and, most importantly, connecting with other women buoyed Sophie's confidence and attitude about her challenging cancer treatment. Sharing her story and learning strategies all but guaranteed Sophie's successful, though complicated, cancer treatment. She needed to continue taking medication and meet with her oncologist for follow-up visits. Moments of darkness came, but when they did, Sophie had the tools and support to return her to the light. Her experience resulted in a new appreciation of the preciousness of each moment and a heightened awareness of what mattered most.

She shared, "One thing's for sure: life as I knew it will never be the same. The physical changes I've undergone are reminders of my inner transformation. The scars may be unsightly, but they are my badges of courage. These days I find myself appreciating the simplest things—a meal with my family, a walk with a friend, reading a good book. Money and material possessions don't mean the same thing to me as they used to. I just need to be surrounded by love and authenticity."

Having learned so much on this journey, Sophie wanted to give back to other women going through cancer treatment. She started volunteering at the local hospital and eventually began to lead her own breast cancer support groups. She was grateful for the opportunity to "pay it forward," providing support to women suffering the trauma associated with a breast cancer diagnosis. Helping others also strengthened her ability to manage her own fear of this insidious disease. Sophie knew firsthand that there was no benefit to grieving alone and that her healing process was promoted by dealing with her grief head-on.

CHAPTER SEVEN
Trapped Between Generations

Jasmine

Jasmine's New York accent was instantly detectable when we spoke on the phone to arrange her initial consultation. She explained that her internist had given her my name when she mentioned feeling unusually depressed. She had recently become an "empty nester" at the same time that her mother, Violet, was diagnosed with Alzheimer's.

As Jasmine entered my office for her first session, her sleek physique and flawless chocolate-brown complexion belied her fifty-nine years. She strode gracefully across the room, perched herself on the couch, and began filling me in on some of her history.

Jasmine shared that some thirty years ago she met her soul mate, Louis. After almost ten years of building careers and traveling together, they decided to settle down and start a family. Their son, Jackson, was now twenty-one and a senior in college, and their daughter, Tasha, was nineteen and entering her sophomore year. Although Jasmine felt the sense of loss that so often accompanies the "empty nest," she also anticipated this being a liberating and joyful phase of her life. While she and Louis would miss the children, and knew they were certainly not through with their responsibilities to them, they were primed to enjoy their newfound freedom.

Current research[16] shows that marital satisfaction does indeed improve when the children finally take leave, as couples experience less stress and have the opportunity to experience more quality time together.

Then came her mother's Alzheimer's diagnosis. Jasmine was filled with worry, yet she also found herself feeling resentful, and for that she felt shame. Jasmine wondered how she had not seen this coming, so that she could have better managed her expectations. This whirlwind of emotion is what brought her into therapy.

Jasmine had considered therapy years earlier, following the untimely and tragic death of her father, but never followed through as she saw herself as someone who was strong and smart, and capable of handling her problems on her own. However, this time she could not sleep or concentrate at work, and had become increasingly anxious and irritable. The sense of loss she experienced as a result of becoming an empty nester, coupled with the unpredictable demands of caring for her mother while working full-time, proved to be more than she could handle without some professional assistance.

With the children successfully launched, Jasmine was poised to pursue personal interests long put on hold. She imagined that she and Louis would finally have time together to reignite their marriage, renew friendships, and travel. This was to be their time.

Jasmine shared, "My mother's decline was gradual at first. She used to ask me the same question ten times and still forget the answer. Sometimes she'd mix up my name with my sister's or forget to close the front door. Then it became more serious. She would leave the stove on and wander off aimlessly in the street. At times, she didn't recognize friends and family, or she would confuse them with relatives who died long ago. She had moments of lucidity when it was hard to imagine anything was seriously wrong, but those moments never lasted.

"I knew when it came time, it would be up to me to care for my mother. My sister, Willa, was so overwhelmed with her own life. She couldn't take on anything more. Her husband had a stroke a few years

---

[16] https://www.ncbi.nlm.nih.gov/pmc/articles/PMC3061469/ (accessed January 10, 2017).

ago that left him wheelchair-bound, and he has a multitude of other complicated medical issues. Louis and I were clearly the best candidates to care for my mother.

"I would have preferred that my mother live with us, but she needed more attention than Louis and I could provide. Eventually, she couldn't bathe or dress herself or even go to the bathroom unassisted. She fell out of bed more than once. We knew she would be safer in a facility with full-time supervision and medical attention. About a year ago, we moved her into a medically based retirement facility close to our home. It's a beautiful place with first-rate care. I visit her every day after work and do whatever I can to help. It's a good place for her because she loves playing card games, singing, and socializing, and this facility is ideal for that. She's managed to make a small network of friends there. She seems to be happy enough, but I still feel guilty about her being in a facility.

"Occasionally, she tells me she's ready to go home. It breaks my heart. She does not comprehend that her place has been sold and that she is never going home. Recently, she's been talking about her mommy, who's been dead for over two decades. It's so sad."

Jasmine described her mother as having been "an expressive and feisty force of nature." She was now a shadow of her former self. It was as if the mother Jasmine knew and loved was slowly being erased. Her personality had all but disappeared, yet her body was very much alive and in need of care. At the beginning, Jasmine maintained the fantasy that her mother would return to her, if only for brief periods. Eventually, she began to accept the harsh reality that her mother's decline was irreversible. She prayed that her mother would not suffer long in this diminished state. Jasmine was in emotional turmoil as she witnessed her mother's deeply disturbing decline.

Self-Preservation

During one of our sessions, Jasmine seemed particularly agitated and weary. She said, "I thought Louis and I would be able to find the time to be together and have some pleasure, even while caring for my mother. This is definitely not the case. I know this sounds selfish, but sometimes, rather than feeling sad for my mother, I find myself filled with anger and resentment. I hate myself for feeling this way, but so much of our time is devoted to her, and these precious years are just slipping away.

"Louis and I have put our dreams on hold again, and it's creating an unspoken tension between us. We just keep doing what's expected of us. There are no good answers and no words to describe the way this hideous disease is consuming my mother." Jasmine welled up but continued to speak through her tears: "I feel like I am constantly running on empty. I need something to look forward to, something that will bring joy, even while dealing with my mother's disintegration. I'm beginning to feel like I have nothing left to give."

Care for the Caregiver

Jasmine's role of caregiver was clearly taking a toll on her psychological well-being and her marriage. Caring for her mother was exhausting and heartbreaking. She was burning out and needed to take better care of herself before her own health began to suffer.

We talked about implementing mindfulness practices. I felt that Jasmine would immediately benefit from the breathing and meditation strategies, helping her to destress and shift her thoughts to a more positive perspective.

She readily took to abdominal breathing and used this technique while driving and whenever she felt the first hints of frustration or stress. Again, with the focus on the breath, I taught her meditation, which I knew she could practice during her visits with her mother. Violet would sleep for long stretches of time, and rather than reading or spacing out, Jasmine could practice meditation and straightaway begin reaping the physical, mental, and emotional benefits.

Over the next few sessions, we reviewed and built upon the breathing and meditation skills. Jasmine began a routine of abdominal breathing in the constructive-rest position at night—especially when she struggled with sleep. Even on those nights when she could not sleep well, in the morning she noticed feeling more rested and relaxed. Jasmine began feeling more present and less resentful with her mother and with her current situation. Slowly, her irritability and anger began to subside.

Creating Space

I thought it might be useful to add to her repertoire of skills a visualization technique called *creating space*. The Buddhist monk and teacher Phakchok Rinpoche developed this method. He contends that inner happiness—that sense of ease, joy, and well-being—does not depend on external circumstances, but rather hinges on our ability to create an open and spacious mind. In response to the worries and demands of life, our minds can become narrow and negative. We become overwhelmed and start to feel trapped. When we create a feeling of spaciousness in the mind and heart, problems seem smaller and less significant. Rinpoche explains that by visualizing spaciousness and allowing the mind to blend into that vast space, we can generate a sense of calm, clarity, and perspective.

This strategy can be practiced alone or in combination with meditation. Jasmine was eager and already primed, having mastered breathing and meditation. I invited her to "sit comfortably on the couch; close your eyes or leave them partially open, whichever feels better. Take a few abdominal breaths to settle the mind and body. Now imagine that you are surrounded by empty space in all directions. Imagine the vastness of this space everywhere. There are no boundaries, no walls, no furniture, no buildings—just open space. When your mind wanders away from this focus, gently bring your attention back, without judgment or criticism. Visualize your mind and heart blending into this space, so that it becomes just as vast and open. Allow yourself to remain in this place of spaciousness for about five to ten minutes, and when you are ready, open your eyes and notice how you feel."

Creating-Space Strategy

- Sit in a comfortable position with your spine supported.

- Close your eyes and take a few abdominal breaths to relax the mind and body.

- Think about and visualize creating space around you, and allow this image to expand.

- Imagine your mind and heart becoming vast and open.

- When your mind wanders, gently bring your attention back to creating space.

- Continue to breathe deeply as you visualize the vastness that surrounds you.

- Allow yourself to relax in this state of mind for several minutes.

- When you are ready, gradually open your eyes.

- Notice how you feel.

This technique can be practiced anywhere, at any time.

Jasmine became aware of feeling a sense of relief in her chest. She said that when she imagined this kind of spaciousness in her mind and heart, she did not feel as stuck and her problems did not seem as overwhelming. With practice, I knew she would be able to create more mental and emotional space to deal with her mother, her marriage, and her work, and find more personal time.

Jasmine began a regular practice of abdominal breathing and meditation, which she often coupled with the creating-space strategy. Whenever she found herself feeling pressured or stressed, she immediately thought about creating space, even when she couldn't tear herself away for a full practice session. She said, "Amazingly, even just the idea of creating space around me calms me down and opens my heart in a way that I have not experienced before. It stops me from feeling trapped. I felt like such a bad person when my anger overwhelmed my love for my mother. Lately, I feel so much love and compassion for her. Ironically, I feel as though I have more time and space for myself these days." Obviously, these strategies did not affect the progression of her mother's illness, but they allowed Jasmine to feel more in control of her reactions as she carried on.

The Unplanned Transition

Good or bad, life is about managing transitions. Nothing in our lives is permanent. Our bodies, our relationships, our world are in a constant state of flux. Yet most of us tend to resist change, preferring to cling to the familiar, which ultimately leads to suffering. Learning to accept change and develop a greater capacity for resilience in the face of transition creates unique opportunities for growth. Each transition presents us with something we must let go of, and something we must embrace. Even when the change is positive, like a move to a new home, a marriage, a birth, or a new job, it is normal to feel sad, confused, angry, afraid, or even numb. As we let go, detaching from our old way of life, and summon the courage to face the unknown, we create the space for our new life to take root.

Jasmine and Louis were excited by their new status as "empty nesters." Life then handed them another challenge they had not anticipated. Their plans were put on hold as they adapted to the demanding role of caring for Jasmine's disabled mother.

For many baby boomers, the empty-nest phase becomes additionally complicated when it is coupled with another life-cycle event, such as caring for aging parents. Conversations regarding the children, work, and future plans are quickly replaced with heart-to-hearts about the challenges of caring for aging and ailing parents.

The Power of Resilience

Resilience is the remarkable quality that allows people knocked down by life to adapt and rise quickly. We all feel grief, sadness, and a range of other painful emotions during times of adversity and loss.

Going through a difficult life transition might feel like a free fall at first, but with resilience, we get back on the path. Resilience comes naturally to some, but most of us need to learn to strengthen this quality in ourselves.

Incorporating certain behavioral strategies deepens one's capacity for resilience. For example, breathing and mindfulness skills help us to be present and assess challenging situations with clarity. These strategies empower us to make better decisions and to bounce back from setbacks. Perhaps the most powerful factor in maximizing resilience is that of surrounding ourselves with caring relationships. Tapping into our support system bolsters confidence and problem-solving abilities, and helps us to manage difficult emotions and impulses. Developing resilience is a personal journey that involves using those strategies that best help us to feel strong and connected.

Managing Multiple Demands

The question arises when the children leave home and our parents need our help, "How do I adjust to my empty nest and the demands of aging parents and still find time to care for myself?" Many adult children feel they do not have the time or energy to care for their own needs during this challenging period. However, self-care, support, and mindfulness strategies are all crucial to the successful navigation of this complicated time of life.

Jasmine continued to need support as she struggled to reconcile her own needs and responsibilities with those of her ailing mother. Several months into our work together, she arrived for her usual session shortly after a visit with her mother. She was unusually agitated and blurted out, "I don't know what to say or how to feel. I can't take the vacant eyes, the confusion, and the disappearance of my once vibrant mother. Her body is here, but she is gone. I can't stand seeing her like this. I know this is horrible to say, and I would never say this anywhere else, but sometimes I wish my mother would die." Jasmine gasped in disbelief, shaking her head in dismay at the words that just came from her mouth. "*What kind of monster am I?*" She whispered. My heart broke for her pain and for the conflict she articulated with such honesty and vulnerability.

People who reveal the secret wish that their ailing parent would die are expressing the thoughts of many caregivers. These are good, decent people who love their failing elder, but who also feel overwhelmed and underequipped to manage the complexities of their loved one's care. Faced with juggling so many conflicting responsibilities, it is not unusual for caregivers to become depressed or burned out.

Silence filled the office as Jasmine's eyes welled with tears and she covered her face in shame. "I didn't mean that. It's just so hard and there is no hope."

"It's okay to feel whatever you are feeling," I reassured her. "Having these thoughts does not make you a bad person. Witnessing your mother's deterioration is challenging, as well as emotionally and physically exhausting. Both you and Louis had such high expectations for this time in your life, and your mother's illness has kept you tethered to her with no idea of how long you will need to care for her. Your life feels like it is not your own, but you can choose to take charge of the way you lead your life, even during this difficult time.

"It is important for you and Louis to continue to care for your mother, but you also need to carve out time for yourselves. Think about spending at least one hour a day nurturing yourself in ways that are meaningful to you. You do not have to wait for your mother to be gone to start caring for yourself. Perhaps you can occasionally skip a day or two of visiting your mom. Think about going to the gym or out to dinner, signing up for a class together, taking a day trip, or doing something that would simply feel pleasurable and relaxing. This nonstop work is beginning to take a toll on your own health, and perhaps your marriage as well. You need to nurture yourself more consistently or you are going to end up ill."

I encouraged Jasmine to teach Louis abdominal breathing and meditation and recommended that they practice together when possible. The breathing and the meditation would bring them more into the present moment and make them better able to accept "what is" with clarity and grace. The visualization practice, I thought, would be best practiced separately, so they could each focus on individual dreams and goals.

Over the next few months, Jasmine found ways to create more space for herself. She joined the choir at her church, a welcoming community of people, with whom she could enjoy her love of singing and music. She and Louis began attending a church group that met every other week for Bible study and a communal dinner. Besides attending to her spiritual well-being, Jasmine began to take twice-weekly Zumba classes and daily morning walks. She realized she needed to take control of her life now, not later.

With these supports and forms of self-care in place, Jasmine began to feel less depleted by the care of her mother. Soon thereafter, she wanted to switch gears in her treatment and share more about her father.

Self-Nurture While Caring for an Ailing Parent

- Seek out support. Your emotional health is not a luxury. It is vital to feel emotionally supported to be an able and effective caregiver. Consider seeking out the help of a professional if need be. Burnout occurs when a caretaker's needs go unmet. Each of us needs assistance to get through challenging times.

- Care for yourself physically. Do what you can to get enough sleep, rest, exercise, and good nutrition. Do not be last on your to-do list.

- Build alone time into your schedule. Meditate, daydream, commune with nature, visit a museum or library. Rejuvenate yourself so that you feel refreshed and have the strength to carry on without resentment.

- Participate in a group. Ideally, join a group of people facing similar circumstances or one that feels meaningful in other ways.

- You might also consider joining a group or taking a class that brings you pleasure, such as music, dance, theater, singing, mah-jongg, or a book group.

Jasmine Reflects on Her Father

Jasmine had previously told me about the tragic car accident that had prematurely taken her father's life. I asked her to tell me more details and its effect on her.

She shared, "My father died twenty years ago this autumn. He was driving with my mother when there was a sudden torrential downpour and the car hydroplaned into a concrete barrier. My father died instantly. My mother suffered a fractured neck, and the prognosis was poor. Miraculously, she survived, but was in a coma for some time and required multiple surgeries.

"About two weeks after the funeral, my mother regained consciousness, and my sister and I mustered the courage to tell her the hideous news. It was terrible. Her world shattered. However, we were all amazed and grateful that after several months of physical therapy, my mother pushed through the physical and emotional pain to recover her health.

"His death was traumatic for all of us, although my mother was the most devastated. She mourned for a long time, and I think she never stopped missing him. My parents did everything together. They were old-fashioned, were religious, and had a strong connection to their community. My mother was strong, but she had always followed my father's lead. It took her a long time to adjust to the permanence of his death.

"I was in my early thirties when he died. Before that, I don't recall anything else rocking my world. I guess I should consider myself lucky for that. His death changed everything for me in such a profound way."

As Jasmine experienced, it is never easy to adjust to the unexpected, traumatic loss of a loved one. We all heal at our own pace. There is no "normal" amount of time for the grieving process; it takes what it takes. In most cases the trauma of loss fades, but the bond with those we love endures forever.

Jasmine recalled her mother's recovery from her grief. She continued, "I remember at one point telling my mother that my sister and I needed her—we wanted her to be a role model for us, her daughters. My mother somehow understood, and she pulled herself together. She began focusing her energy on the family. She reengaged with her friends, played bridge, became more involved with her church, and baked and cooked endlessly for every possible occasion."

I asked, "What kind of man was your father?"

"He was a good person, patient and soft-spoken. I felt closer to him than to my mother, because he always found time for me. He made me feel important. My father talked with me for hours about school, future plans, friends, everything. On the other hand, my mother was always planning, cooking, and organizing. She told me what to do, but she was constantly busy and we didn't have many serious conversations.

"My father supported me in developing a professional life, even though it was less common for a girl, especially a black girl, to have those aspirations back then. He was traditional in many ways, but forward-thinking when it came to a woman's need for education and finding meaning beyond family life. I'm grateful he gave that to me.

"I'll never forget the phone call from the hospital when they told me he died. My whole world changed in that instant. I walked around in a daze that entire first day. It was like my life was moving in slow motion. For years, I used to dream about my father almost nightly. Now he only visits my dreams occasionally. In my dreams, he's always talking to me and I'm so happy. Then I wake up and remember he's gone. Still, those dreams have been important to me and have offered me wise counsel at times. I don't think I've ever fully gotten over his death."

Dreams of loved ones who have died are a natural part of the grieving process and can help us heal. They might occur shortly after the death of a loved one or years later. Jasmine's dreams about her father kept him alive in her mind, especially when she looked for guidance. She knew deep down that her bond with her father would endure forever. Jasmine would ask him for help during difficult times, and she would imagine how he would have counseled her.

I suggested, "Perhaps you can seek counsel from him about how to best manage this time of your life in one of your meditations or in your imagination." Jasmine nodded.

Over the next few months, Jasmine continued to talk about her father, her mother, her childhood, her loves, and her losses. Her mother's decline progressed and Jasmine's daily visits continued. Simultaneously, her creativity during this difficult time began to emerge. Jasmine shared how she and Louis were finding ways to honor her mother but still move forward in their own lives.

Recharging a Marriage Through Communication

On weekends, Louis and Jasmine began taking Violet, in her wheelchair, to social gatherings they would have previously missed. They usually stayed only an hour or two before she got cranky, but in that time they reconnected with friends. Jasmine continued singing in the choir and getting together with her women friends. Louis began playing guitar again, which he had not done in over twenty years. They were beginning to find opportunities for pleasure, even in the throes of their demanding lives.

Strategies to Improve Communication with Your Partner

- Listen. Listen. Listen. Listening is one of the most powerful ways to become a better communicator with your partner. Often, incorrectly, we assume that we know what the other person will say. When your partner feels truly heard, he or she will feel more valued and less defensive.

- Restate what your partner shares. Make sure that you understand by repeating the message in your own words.

- Learn to tolerate strong emotional responses. When in the throes of a difficult conversation, practice breathing techniques. This will help you to stay calm and present.

- Be compassionate. Think about the way you speak with your partner. Speak in a manner that is respectful and likely to encourage open, honest communication.

- Bring your authentic self to the dialogue. Partners know when the other person is being false or sarcastic, and it breaks down communication quickly. Authenticity promotes healthy conversation, however painful the topic.

- Plan regular alone time for conversation and intimacy. Create a ritual of spending time together without interference from children, pets, or electronics.

- Resolve conflicts fairly. No one wins unless both partners are treated fairly and get at least some of what they need.

- Forgive the disappointments and mistakes of your partner. Research shows that forgiveness is best for the health of the person doing the forgiving.[17] Even when a situation cannot be resolved, it is good to forgive so that you can let go and move on.

- Schedule fun activities together. Remember what brought you together. Build on the strengths of the relationship. Spend time with couples who have healthy relationships and learn from their behavior.

According to relationship experts John and Julie Gottman, happy couples behave like good friends, and they handle their conflicts in gentle, positive ways.[18] They are able to successfully repair negative interactions during an argument, and they process negative emotions fully. Jasmine and Louis were beginning to redefine the terms of their

[17] http://www.hopkinsmedicine.org/health/healthy_aging/healthy_connections/ forgiveness-your-health-depends-on-it (accessed January 10, 2017).

[18] John M. Gottman, Julie Gottman, and Joan DeClaire, *Ten Lessons to Transform Your Marriage: America's Love Lab Experts Share Their Strategies for Strengthening Your Relationship* (New York: Harmony Books, 2007).

marriage according to their individual needs as well as their shared goals as a couple. They communicated well, listening reflectively to what the other person expressed, and did what they could to ensure each other's happiness. This extended into the intimacy of their sex lives. Jasmine and Louis had joyfully renewed and reinvigorated this aspect of their marriage—an outgrowth of strengthened communication and a heightened sense of closeness.

During one of our conversations, Jasmine relayed that she had been practicing meditation and felt less burned out and more present. She also reported feeling more connected to Louis and to her friends. She added, however, that she still felt a nagging sense of emptiness and a feeling that she had been cheated in life. She hated feeling this way and wanted some help to overcome those feelings.

The Secret Power of Gratitude

We talked about how and why Jasmine felt cheated. It was centered on the traumatic loss of her father, being saddled with the bulk of caring for her mother, watching her mother's personality disappear even as her body lived on, and not having the time to travel and pursue her own later-in-life dreams. The stress she was under seemed to exacerbate a tendency to focus on the negative, burdensome parts of her life. She failed to give equal focus to the fact that she'd had good, loving parents, and that she had wonderful and accomplished children, a devoted partner, a job she valued, great health, and the potential to fulfill many of her dreams in the coming years. Instead, she was fixated on the limitations and the loss of freedom in becoming her mother's caregiver.

Jasmine's negative perspective was keeping her stuck. Minimizing the good in her life prevented her from finding more joy. She needed to change some of her negative thoughts and begin to build a more positive outlook. To do so, Jasmine had to cultivate and internalize the ability to be grateful for all that was good in her life. I suggested she learn a simple gratitude strategy that would help her change her perspective.

Gratitude and Psychology

Martin Seligman and his colleagues launched the field of *positive psychology* about twenty years ago and began scientifically studying emotions such as gratitude, optimism, forgiveness, happiness, and altruism. At the time, this was a revolutionary idea in the field of psychology since most of the data about human emotion had previously focused on aspects of psychology related to problems, deficits, and pathology, such as mental illness, trauma, addiction, and stress. Developing positive attributes leads to greater happiness and resilience, and fortifies us during times of adversity and emotional turmoil.

Gratitude is a basic human emotion that is about our ability to feel and express thankfulness and appreciation. Traditionally, the study of this emotion has been relegated to the fields of theology and philosophy. In 2007, Robert Emmons began researching gratitude through a psychological lens. He found that integrating gratitude into one's consciousness improves mental and physical well-being, quality of sleep, and the overall experience of happiness, and these effects tend to be long-lasting.[19]

Cultivating Gratitude

The most common method for cultivating gratitude is by keeping a *gratitude journal* and recording experiences for which one is grateful. The idea is to write about at least three positive experiences on a daily basis. Examples include taking notice of something in nature, an object of beauty, a pleasant conversation with a friend, a good cup of coffee, or helping someone with a problem. Recording these positive experiences has been shown to boost levels of alertness, enthusiasm, determination, attentiveness, and energy, especially when compared to those who recorded or focused on negative events.[20] Our days rarely go according to plan or without unexpected challenges. Some of us can naturally

---

[19] Robert A. Emmons, *Thanks!: How the New Science of Gratitude Can Make You Happier* (Boston: Houghton Mifflin Harcourt, 2007).

[20] http://ei.yale.edu/wp-content/uploads/2013/11/jclp22020.pdf (accessed January 10, 2017).

appreciate the sweet moments as they happen throughout the day, while many of us need to cultivate this sense of appreciation.

I asked Jasmine to keep a daily gratitude journal, and she willingly agreed. She was already in the habit of journaling periodically, but the gratitude journal was intended only for writing down those events for which she felt appreciation. The idea was for Jasmine to focus on the nuances of her day and observe those experiences that brought her even a moment of joy or delight. She began to cultivate the part of her brain that encouraged her to think more optimistically, to feel happier and more satisfied with her life, and to build on positive emotions.

I also encouraged her to say "thank you" to others while looking them in the eyes. It seemed important that she connect with others while learning to be authentically grateful. Using a simple "thank you" is a way of recognizing and honoring others. The meta-message of this everyday expression is that "I see you, you matter, and we are connected." When this connection is made through a simple "thank you," both giver and receiver feel valued and visible. Showing appreciation acknowledges another human being and honors the interrelationship between "I" and "thou."

Some days felt more challenging than others for Jasmine, but eventually she found a way to tease out the moments for which she truly felt grateful. Over time, she noticed herself feeling more optimistic, happy, and open-minded, and less resentful. She felt a greater sense of connectedness and noticed a qualitative difference in her mood as well as in her sleep.

I decided to build on this gratitude strategy by teaching Jasmine a technique known as taking in the good, developed in 2009 by Rick Hanson. He explains that our thoughts have the power to shape our brains.[21] The more conscious we are about perceiving an event as being good or "good enough," the more this positive perception will generalize to other parts of our brain. However, Hanson explains that negative experiences are like Velcro and tend to stick in our minds, whereas

---

[21] Rick Hanson, *Buddha's Brain: The Practical Neuroscience of Happiness, Love & Wisdom* (Oakland, CA: New Harbinger Publications, Inc., 2009).

positive experiences are like Teflon and more readily slip away. We must actively work to integrate positive experiences into the brain in order for the beneficial effects to endure. The question remains, how do we do this?

There are several basic steps to taking in the good, all of which echo the practices of relaxation, visualization, meditation, and self-hypnosis. The specific purpose of this strategy is to weave positive emotions, optimism, and resilience into the brain and the self. I have made a few suggestions to add to the technique described by Dr. Hanson.

Learning to take in the good and truly savor positive experiences may be a bit challenging at first, but it will get easier and more "Velcro-like" with practice.

Taking-in-the-Good Strategy

- Choose a comfortable seated position.

- Take a few abdominal breaths, relaxing the mind and body.

- Look for positive facts in your life and/or traits about yourself.

- Expand upon each positive fact or trait, turning it into a "positive experience."

- Savor the memory of this experience for a minute or so; involve all of your senses.

- Intensify this feeling even further for an additional minute.

- Allow this positive feeling to soak deeply into the recesses of your mind and body.

- Continue building a repertoire of positive experiences.

- The longer something is held in conscious awareness, the more it becomes embedded in the brain.

Jasmine responded well to this strategy of learning to appreciate the positive in her life. The gratitude journaling helped, but this practice of "taking in the good" somehow felt more immediate and compelling. She noticed that her time with her failing mother became more meaningful and precious. The resentment she had previously felt slowly dissolved into a greater capacity for patience and compassion. In short order, Jasmine began savoring the moments with her mother, and her attitude was contagious. Louis followed suit and he, too, began to cherish this time with the last parent left in their family.

The Call

One Sunday evening, I got "the call" from Jasmine. Her mother had died peacefully in her bed earlier that day. We met the following morning. Jasmine's face was puffy from a sleepless night of tears.

"I always thought it would feel different, easier. She hasn't really been 'there' for so long. I thought it would be a relief. But in the past months, I'd begun to appreciate my mother in a way I never had before. I liked seeing her on her good or bad days. Just being with her reminded me of all the times she stood by me when I was growing up. She took such good care of me, fussing over me when I was sick, cooking my favorite meals when I came home from school, whispering to me when I couldn't sleep. She did so much and endured so much. I can't believe she's gone."

Jasmine shook in grief and spent the rest of the session talking about the time she spent caring for her mother, her mother's idiosyncrasies, her passion for baking, her love for her girls and for Jasmine's father. As the enormity of the loss sank in, she was thankful that she had Louis to help her through her grief.

Toward the end of our session she told me, "Louis and I have been preparing for this, so my mother's affairs and the funeral arrangements are all in order. My sister and several of my friends will make the calls." Jasmine paused for a while and continued, "No more parents. No more buffers between death and me.

"As Baptists, we are supposed to believe in heaven. I go to church and I pray, but I've always had trouble knowing exactly what to believe when it came to life after death. My mother believed. I guess that's important.

Before her mind started to go, she told me that upon her death she wanted us to celebrate the life she had lived rather than to focus the funeral on her being gone. She believed that, at last, she would be joining my father in heaven. I don't know if my faith is that defined, but I know we will celebrate her life in church."

A week later, when Jasmine and I next met, the most vivid memory she shared from her mother's funeral service was the hundreds of flowers, mostly pink roses, which were her mother's favorite flower, that were sent by all those who had known and loved her. Her mother's closed casket had been draped with a white linen cloth and topped with her parents' wedding portrait, displayed in a beautiful silver frame. The music and hymns stirred Jasmine's heart and reminded her of so many touching moments with her mother. Many who attended the service spoke to Jasmine of their own sweet memories, and it all helped Jasmine feel more at peace with her mother's passing.

Jasmine spent the next months mourning the loss of her mother and her father. She revealed many recollections: the way her parents interacted and treated Jasmine and her sister, their family traditions, their clashes, their passions. She shared story after story, releasing her grief with each telling.

The Value of Ritual

I suggested to Jasmine that she create some ritual around the loss of her mother. Rituals punctuate significant moments and transitions in our lives and can foster deep healing as they bring meaning, comfort, and order to our lives, especially during difficult times. They can be private and deeply personal or shared with others. What we cherish is celebrated and remembered in a predictable way, and this gives us a feeling of normalcy and control. Grief rituals are usually spawned from religious or family traditions, but can also be one's own unique creation.

Jasmine incorporated some of these rituals and found them helpful in her grieving process. Eventually, she began to talk about her own mortality and her wish to live her life fully, as never before. She shared, "I have a long list of experiences I want to have in the coming years, both with Louis and on my own. There isn't time to do everything, so I need to prioritize and get going."

Rituals to Honor a Loved One

- Create a memory book or a collage of photographs.

- Share personal stories from your loved one's life.

- Light candles on anniversaries or when you are feeling the loss.

- Bring plants or flowers to the gravesite.

- Gather friends to take part in an evening to honor your loved one.

- Go to your place of worship to say mourning prayers.

- Help others in honor of your loved one.

- Imagine engaging in a conversation with your loved one and visualize his or her response.

- Write a letter to complete anything left unsaid or to say your goodbyes.

The reality was that the mourning process was taking longer than Jasmine had anticipated. She shared with me that sometimes she would miss her mother when she passed by a bakery, heard a bird chirping, smelled roses in bloom, or, of course, when she looked at old photographs and videos. Slowly, she began to emerge from her grief.

Jasmine and Louis began to travel. They made their way to Italy, Greece, and several islands. While she loved these trips, something was still lacking. She hungered to find greater depth and meaning in her adventures and in her work, and pleasure travel simply did not satisfy that need.

During one of our sessions, she told me, "I've been thinking about my legacy, about what I want to do with the rest of my life that will have a lasting effect after I'm gone. My parents' passing has made me appreciate the transience of life and how vulnerable we all are. I've had this revelation that my desire for adventure must be combined with helping others and giving back."

Over the next year, Jasmine became a leader in fund-raising events, helping a variety of nonprofit organizations in her community. In particular, she became passionate about helping a women's shelter for victims of domestic abuse. She could not bear the fact that so many women in the United States and around the world suffered from domestic violence. Jasmine found her calling in her efforts on behalf of underserved and victimized girls and women. She wanted to first make a difference locally and then take her concerns for abused women to a wider, more global platform.

Altruism

Jasmine had stumbled upon the practice of altruism. She did not have much prior experience giving to others in this way, but after the death of her mother she felt compelled to explore it. Initially she did not know where to begin, but quickly discovered volunteer opportunities. These small contributions of her time and energy developed into leadership roles where Jasmine began organizing major fund-raising initiatives.

Altrusim is defined as unselfish regard for or devotion to the welfare of others. It is often thought to be an act of self-sacrifice for the benefit of others. Another way to think about altruism is as a generous way of expressing gratitude for all that we have. Research shows that altruism, like gratitude, is strongly associated with health, happiness, and overall well-being.[22] Altruism is a trait that can be cultivated with training and practice. Helping others and performing acts of loving kindness leads to a cascade of positive emotions, including increased vitality and heightened self-esteem. Among its potential benefits, altruism is believed to:
  • Enhance physical and emotional well-being
  • Reduce stress, anger, and their negative effects

---

[22] Stephen G. Post, "Altruism, Happiness, and Health: It's Good to Be Good," *International Journal of Behavioral Medicine* 12, no. 2 (June 2005): 66–77.

- Help combat addiction
- Boost mood, happiness, and self-esteem
- Diminish anxiety, depression, and pain
- Foster healing, fight disease, and increase longevity
- Provide feelings of gratification and inner warmth known as "helper's high"
- Stimulate a ripple effect of generosity throughout the community
- Deepen social connection, allowing one to feel part of the greater whole

How to Cultivate Altruism

- Commit to making a difference in the lives of others.
- Practice compassion meditation, which focuses on easing the suffering of others.
- Keep an altruism journal about the ways in which you make a difference.
- Visualize being of service.
- Draw upon your own unique gifts and talents to make a difference.
- Help someone at least once a day.
- Pay attention to the news, and within your limits give generously to those in need.
- Discuss with others the value of giving. Give something, even in hard times.
- Know that helping others benefits you *and* changes the world.

Jasmine's efforts to serve neglected and violated girls and women grew as she continued her volunteer efforts. Her deepest wish was to work with her global "girlfriends" in Africa. She wanted to make a difference in the land of her ancestors. Jasmine had never spoken of this dream, as it had seemed so distant and unattainable. No longer. She decided to take a sabbatical from work to travel for several months to various parts of Africa. Jasmine planned to volunteer for humanitarian relief agencies that helped traumatized girls and women recover from atrocities such as human trafficking and sexual slavery. This mission became her singular passion. She was determined to make a difference in Africa, one girl and one woman at a time.

There were so many opportunities that lay before Jasmine; her world was exploding with possibility. I was moved to hear about all she was learning and planning. In our two years of work together, Jasmine moved from feeling trapped and helpless to fully embracing her personal power and sense of purpose.

The Next Stage of Life

I applauded Jasmine's enthusiasm and energy. She revealed that in recent months she and Louis had felt more connected than ever before. Together, they shared their aspirations for this new phase of their lives. Louis wholeheartedly supported Jasmine's desires and wanted to accompany her on some of her humanitarian trips. His only wish was that she not be gone for more than a month at a time, and to this she readily agreed.

Louis's passion lay more in the arena of music. For years, he longed to play music. He had recently begun practicing in his basement studio and eventually put together a small band. He too was ready for the next step. Louis's dream was to play in local venues and to record his music. Jasmine told me that Louis's deepening involvement in music made her feel proud of him and heightened their intimacy.

Jasmine and Louis negotiated new terms at their respective places of employment so that they could work flexible hours and take more time off. They felt well equipped to confront the inevitable life challenges to come. So many opportunities lay ahead to make a difference in the lives of others, to create a legacy, and to fulfill their long-held dreams.

CHAPTER EIGHT
Beyond the Therapy Door

*B*ehind the Therapy Door: Simple Strategies to Transform Your Life has invited you into the inner sanctum of a psychologist's office and the lives of six courageous women as a way of providing you with the tools necessary to create your best life. The skills offered will support your quest for greater personal insight, happiness, and resilience, and more satisfying relationships. I encourage you to embrace those strategies that are most relevant to you and integrate them into your daily routine.

In review and beyond . . .

The Breath

Learning to breathe abdominally is one of the simplest and most elegant ways to bring ourselves into the present moment, quiet the mind, dissolve stress, and initiate the healing process. The breath lies at the root of all other mindfulness strategies. As we incorporate the use of abdominal breathing, we can stop muscling through difficult moments and begin to incorporate a greater sense of ease and calm. The secret to abdominal breathing is learning to make the breath deeper, slower, quieter, and more rhythmic. The more you practice, the more it will penetrate your conscious and unconscious mind.

When we use the breath as a tool, we also stop resisting. We gain the ability to be with or to tolerate whatever emotions or challenges arise, which leads to greater inner peace and grace. Focusing on the breath can help us to tolerate painful emotions and summon courage at any given moment and break through moments of confusion and darkness.

All other mindfulness methods are powerful adjuncts to the immediacy and accessibility of the breathing techniques. If you can only commit to learning one technique for now, I recommend with all of my heart that you become proficient in the practice of deep, conscious breathing. Every day, regardless of how demanding your schedule may be, there are a multitude of opportunities to practice breathing. The results will be potent and cumulative.

Mindfulness

Mindfulness is purposely paying attention in the present moment to thoughts, feelings, and sensations, without criticism or judgment. This helps to cultivate a quieter mind and the ability to tolerate the rise and fall of emotions, and to develop greater fortitude. Being mindful strengthens and restores energy. It helps us to become awake to our experience, so we remain a calm witness to the joys and sorrows that make up the fabric of our lives. Rather than overreacting to situations as they arise, mindfulness trains us to step back, find greater clarity and insight, and choose the best response to challenge.

The mindfulness strategies in *Behind the Therapy Door* have been presented with specific, concrete instructions. Some of these practices are drawn from ancient traditions and were considered "alternative" methods when I first began my research and clinical work. Today these techniques are being carefully researched and validated using modern science, and in many cases have become mainstream treatment modalities in the arenas of psychology and medicine.

This is a "golden era" for mind-body medicine and cutting-edge psychophysiological research. Advances in technology have illuminated the inextricable connection between the brain and physical and emotional well-being. The mind-body strategies presented here will help you attain greater peace, creativity, compassion, spiritual connection, and personal meaning. These qualities recalibrate your happiness set point and pave the way toward the realization of your goals and dreams.

The Power of Friendship

The stories of Anne, Carolyn, Molly, Melissa, Sophie, and Jasmine exemplify the primary reasons most women come to therapy, which at its essence is to alleviate feelings of stress, loss, abandonment, or alienation. As these women develop their inner resources and such resources become "personally sustainable," they are able to make better choices and establish more gratifying relationships with themselves and with others.

Over the years, I have repeatedly seen that when women learn how to successfully manage their reactions to stress, they become healthier emotionally and physically, and experience a greater sense of empowerment. Their capacity for self-love and maintaining loving and supportive relationships is dramatically enhanced. We now know that we can change the way our brain functions by practicing mindfulness strategies. In this way, we have the ability to train our brains to work for us in the best possible ways. We can learn to heighten awareness, create gratifying relationships, and lead fulfilling lives.

Changing the way the brain "fires" is related to neuroplasticity— the ability of the brain to change consistent with one's experience. This happens over time through the practice of specific approaches that help shape thoughts and behavior. These methods include breathing techniques, meditation and relaxation exercises, prayer, affirmations, conscious eating, exercise, and self-hypnosis—all of which tap into the powers of the mind. Mindfulness strategies have the potential to affect every aspect of our lives. Over time, these practices infiltrate the mind and heart whether we are doing the dishes, speaking with our children, or running our businesses. Once we are on this illuminated path, there is no turning back.

Mindfulness and Friendship

The mindfulness practices discussed in this book are about building a stronger sense of self and more authentic connections with others. As you become more able to quiet your self-critical voice and access your curiosity, self-acceptance, and self-love, you will be more able to do this with the people in your life. It is the quality of our relationships and support systems that bring our greatest sense of pleasure. Mindfulness strategies brought into the context of relationships help us to be fully present with others, and without judgment.

For women, friendships are essential to well-being. They play a crucial role in our lives, providing a unique intimacy that differs from the bonds shared with partners or other family members. Our women friends help shape who we are and who we hope to become. They help us to heal during tumultuous times and offer a unique kind of support that other relationships do not provide. Research repeatedly demonstrates that women are healthiest and happiest when they have good, supportive friendships. There is safety and acceptance in healthy friendships that allow us to tap into the awareness that we are all part of a greater whole. Being able to share from our hearts and reveal our true selves with a circle of loving and supportive friends makes our dreams and intentions seem entirely possible.

Taking in the Good

We have thousands of thoughts each day, and many of these thoughts are the same ones as yesterday and the day before that. Sadly, many of these thoughts are negative, and the more we focus on these thoughts, the stronger they become. Rick Hanson describes this as a "negativity bias." We tend to hang on to negative memories and experiences and allow the positive ones to slip away. Training our brains to savor the good in life rather than perseverating on the negative can shift our attitudes in ways that bring greater contentment. This does not mean that we are chasing the elusive feeling of happiness, but rather that we are training our brains to savor pleasurable moments when they come along.

Taking in the good is about cultivating the ability to embrace joyful experiences. Amid all the sorrow and loss that life brings, it is important to celebrate and appreciate the sweet moments. This helps us build a solid foundation from which other positive thoughts and emotions can emerge. Then, when disappointment or devastation strikes, we have a reservoir of positive experience to help catapult ourselves back into a place of well-being.

With a solid inner foundation and loving relationships, we feel strengthened and are more capable of realizing our full potential, regardless of how we spend our days. We can remove the masks of fear and self-doubt and step into personal, relational, and professional power. This is not to say that our lives will be perfect, but we can embark upon our journey with greater resilience and the capacity to make better choices.

Mindfulness and its inherent higher consciousness help us tap into what is most important with truth and clarity. We understand that we are all connected and that we each have the power to make a difference in each other's lives—one breath at a time.

The Next Step

I encourage you to experiment with the strategies delineated in this book and implement the ones that resonate for you. The configuration of strategies you implement may change occasionally, but whatever form it takes will ultimately guide you to a state of heightened awareness about yourself, your relationships, and the world around you.

With the traumatic events that so many of us have witnessed close to home and around the world in recent years, our collective consciousness needs to heal. We need to make sense of unimaginable losses and tragic events. All of us consciously or unconsciously bear this pain and suffering. Greater mindfulness can ignite our shared purpose to treat others and ourselves with greater kindness, compassion, and purpose. This purpose begins with being present with each other—to reach out, listen with our hearts, and connect with our friends, family, neighbors, colleagues, and beyond. It is our coming together that makes even the most hideous losses seem tolerable. From birth to death, we are bonded with others—past and present—and it behooves us to make these connections as fulfilling as possible.

When we feel whole within ourselves, we release fear and the illusion of being separate. Relationships take on new meaning and become ever more central to our lives. We awaken to the suffering of humankind and summon the strength and compassion to serve others. The ultimate expression of mindfulness is realizing that we are all connected, with each breath and with each action that we take. Thich Nhat Hanh said, "If we are peaceful, if we are happy, we can blossom like a flower, and everyone in our family, our entire society . . . will benefit from our peace."

When we heal ourselves, we heal the world.

CHAPTER NINE
Finding Your Life Purpose

I wanted to take a look at the progression of steps that we zigzag through in order to find our life purpose. *Why are we here? What is it that we are meant for in this one beautiful and precious life of ours?* The journey is by no means linear.

From my perspective as a psychologist in the trenches helping people overcome their most significant challenges for almost four decades, I firmly believe that finding your life purpose begins within the recesses of the self. It is the way we perceive our life experiences and manage ourselves in response to these events.

In this chapter I'd like to examine some of the aspects discussed in this book that can potentially serve as a guiding light for how you proceed in your life.

Being able to self-regulate and self-soothe and having a core foundation in place for when the going gets tough are of paramount importance. The anchor for this foundation is abdominal breathing, along with a regular practice of self-care strategies previously discussed.

In less than thirty minutes a day it's possible to put into place a systematic approach that fosters your emotional stability on any given day, regardless of what comes along. By training your mind and body to become exquisitely familiar with a neutral and calm state of being, you will find that challenges are no longer as demanding or debilitating.

When we bring a more stable and grounded self into our relationships, it makes them more satisfying and provides the potential to discover personal meaning and fulfillment.

How to Discover Your Life Purpose

I suggest you have your journal or pen and paper nearby so that you can respond to some of the questions and exercises presented.

Do you find yourself still searching for your purpose in life?
Do you have clarity about what matters most to you?
What drives you to get up in the morning and claim the day?
What gives you a sense of joy and meaning?
Is what gives you a sense of joy and meaning aligned with the life that you lead day in and day out?
Do you feel a tug toward something bigger—something you can't quite pin down?
Do you wonder what you could do with your life that would be important, that would count—that could bring added value to others and thereby bring greater meaning to your life?

The answers to these questions can be elusive and therefore frustrating to consider. But I encourage you to think about them and give serious consideration to your most heartfelt answers—either now or when you have the opportunity to give this exercise the time it deserves.

We are born with an insatiable curiosity about the world—about why we're here—why there's a sun, moon, and solar system. What's it all about?

Can you remember this sense of wonder when you were a young child? How amazing so many things seemed to you?

If your curiosity was encouraged, you may very well have lived your life seeking answers to what holds the most meaning and value for you, and maybe you discovered your purpose for being.

If your curiosity was ignored or kept under wraps, you likely learned early on to stifle or to repress this natural thirst to explore.

Understanding your purpose helps you find your essence, be true to yourself, and remember what matters in order to live with intention.

Precious few of us know from the get-go what we're meant to do. Often those rare individuals with outstanding talents like great musicians, artists, or scientists know that they were put on this planet to make a difference in those areas.

More often than not, most of us are not so clear about our purpose. The truth is that we do know what calls us—it lies within us—but often it's been interfered with in childhood, stifled by the cascade of the demands of others and subsequently by the adult responsibilities that have become our lives. As a result of these demands and responsibilities, we tend to operate from our heads rather than our hearts—so we don't readily access our heart-centered information.

Discovering your life purpose becomes exquisitely important as we approach or are in the throes of midlife—for this is when the universe gently pulls you in close and whispers, *This is it. No more screwing around. It's time.* It is time to find meaning and joy, and not just on special occasions. It's time to savor the sweetness and move toward personal fulfillment every day of your life as much as possible—because this is it!

Avoiding Regrets

Palliative care nurse Bronnie Ware compiled the "Top five regrets of the dying."[23] I mention them here in the hope that with this knowledge you can reverse-engineer and make the life changes necessary to avoid these regrets at the end of the line:

1. I wish I'd had the courage to live a life true to myself, not the life others expected of me.
2. I wish I had not worked so hard.
3. I wish I'd had the courage to express my feelings.
4. I wish I had stayed in touch with my friends.
5. I wish that I had let myself be happier.

[23] Bronnie Ware, *The Top Five Regrets of the Dying: A Life Transformed by the Dearly Departing* (Carlsbad, CA: Hay House, 2012).

When it comes to making change, be patient and self-compassionate. Each day is an opportunity to move closer to creating a life that nourishes you in profound and authentic ways. It's about moving in the direction of your purpose every day.

What is important to know if you haven't already experienced this—although my guess is that you have—is that even when you're on track with your life purpose, there will be struggles.

Challenges and losses frequently come at the worst possible times, and there may be days when you question whatever you've chosen as your path.

Commitments take sacrifice—which sometimes interferes with other desires and demands. Commitments require being able to ride through the rough patches, staying the course and knowing that nothing is pleasurable all of the time. Finding your life purpose means taking an aerial view of what's most important to you. For example, if you want to be a writer but can't handle rejection, it's likely not going to work out too well for you. If you want to build a business but you can't stand working long hours, then you'll be in trouble there as well.

Initially, most of us are not even necessarily very good at what we love doing, even if it's our passion and life purpose—at least not until we've been at it for some time. Living a life of purpose often means being willing to expose one's imperfect true self. Being willing to be both patient and vulnerable is part of the ride.

If you can't handle the idea of feeling vulnerable, you're likely going to severely limit the possibilities of what you do with your life. Embarrassment and even shame are sometimes part of the process. Putting yourself out there in the name of self-discovery often takes courage and perhaps even a bit of fierceness.

I think of all of the times I've fallen on my face during my career. I recall seeing some of my first patients and "flying by the seat of my pants," as one of my supervisors aptly referred to it. I also remember the terror I experienced the first time I spoke before an auditorium of physicians.

I'd do what I could to shake off the feelings of incompetence and then keep on going. Interestingly, in these many instances of fear and trepidation I also recall those moments in which I knew I had found my groove. A small voice from within assured me that I was on the right path.

Countless other times I'd feel the pain of the seemingly insurmountable challenges and I'd say to myself, *I'm done this time. I can't take the exposure or the endless demands and long hours and hard work.* And yet, I inevitably found myself waking up to a new day realizing that I'm not done and that I have no real choice but to carry on.

What I've learned is that it pretty much doesn't matter exactly what path you choose as your purpose; the most important thing is that you believe in your heart of hearts that you are doing what you know is important to you and makes a difference to others. The research confirms that helping others is indeed the fastest way to happiness and a life of meaning.

On a separate note, consider this: passion requires taking action. It is not a mental activity that somehow summons you through deep thinking or by fortuitous life events. Maybe in a rare instance you manage to stumble upon something that feels meaningful and beckons you. Mostly it's a matter of trial and error, that is, getting going and doing whatever calls you rather than waiting for the sign that says, "This is it!"

Experimentation and practice will let you know that you're doing what you're meant to do. Sometimes you feel it in your heart and sometimes in your gut. Chances are that you have several interests or passions that make you feel as if you're in the right spot. It's like coming home to a place where you know you belong.

Exercise for Finding Your Life Purpose

Imagine that you didn't have a job. You have to be out of the house all day. The kids are grown and independent, and money is not a factor.

- What would you want to do with your time?

- Would you look for a certain kind of work?

- Would you want to travel, and if so, to do what?

- Would you want to volunteer?

- Would you want to sign up for a class or get another degree?

- Would you want to research a particular medical condition or environmental issue and solutions?

- Would you want to explore the globe or learn to fly planes?

- What would move you at this stage of life?

Write your thoughts in your journal and see what you come up with.

Another (perhaps morose, but motivating) way of thinking about this is: if you knew you were going to die in a year, what would you want to do? How would you like to be remembered?

Most of us avoid thinking about death. It's too scary. Yet the truth is that we're all going there, so putting it on the table helps us to prioritize and separate what's most important to us from what's frivolous and distracting. It's helpful to look at each day and sort out what moves you toward certain interests, goals, and passions versus what moves you away from doing what really matters.

After all, each of us possesses our own unique vitality or life force that gets transmitted to the world through our actions. We are working with a force that is deeper than simply making conscious decisions. We are working with the power of destiny. I'd like to distinguish here between destiny and fate. Destiny is that which we actively pursue, whereas fate is that which is inevitable. They dance with each other to create our path.

In essence, discovering one's purpose boils down to opening up to the vitality that flows within your heart and acting upon it. We each become a vessel that contains energy or life force. We can choose to tap into our creativity and discover this force more intimately or remain quietly on the sidelines. When we tune into ourselves in a way that feels harmonious with the deepest forces within us, we feel compelled to do more of the same.

Our heart and body tell us when we are on the right path and when we are open to listening. Wonderful sensations happen in your body when you experience the life you are meant to have. Blood pressure, heart rate, and muscle tension all decrease, breathing becomes slower and more rhythmic, and there will likely be a release of oxytocin and serotonin—both of which are considered "feel-good" hormones.

As you make life changes, remember to check in with your body, for it holds a multitude of secrets that reveal themselves to you when you pay close attention. Also, when you check in with your emotional reality, you will likely find greater inner peace and joy. This doesn't mean that happiness will prevail at all times, but that the general direction of your life feels right.

Visualizing Your Ideal Day

This is an exercise that can help you discover your life purpose and desires with greater clarity and focus. It will help you tune out the responsibilities and expectations that others have of you. The goal is to imagine a single day in your life that is representative of how you might envision yourself living five years from now.

If at any point during this exercise no images come to mind or you drift to someplace else for a while, don't worry. When this happens, go back to your breath and then back to the directions. There is no judgment for however this plays out for you. It will all be grist for the mill.

Choose a comfortable sitting or lying position where you can relax without interruption. You may wish to keep a pen and paper nearby so that you can jot down ideas that emerge as you go through this process.

- Begin by taking several deep belly breaths in and out. Relax your body completely, either in the chair that you're sitting in or on the surface that's supporting you.
- Starting from the head and moving to the toes, we'll do a *body scan*. Relax your scalp so the muscle sheath that composes your scalp is slackened.
- Then relax all of your facial muscles, especially the little muscles around your eyes and jaws. Part your lips slightly and relax your jaw, your mouth, and your tongue. Your face is serene and expressionless.
- Feel your neck and shoulders releasing. Your shoulders are falling directly over your torso. Feel your upper, middle, and lower back lie into the chair. Feel your buttocks and backs of your upper legs supported by the chair or the surface that you're on.
- Begin letting go even more deeply. Enjoy feeling grounded and comfortable.
- Now, traveling down your legs to your feet, feel the support of the floor and the earth beneath the floor, so that your whole body is relaxed and comfortably held.
- Continue to breathe *in* and breathe *out* at your own pace as you move through this exercise—without changing or manipulating your breathing pattern. Just allow the natural rise and fall of your breath to happen.
- Allow yourself to be fully present with whatever you're feeling in your body.

Tune into your senses rather than your thoughts. Allow your senses to take hold: taste, touch, sight, sound, and smell.

Just let yourself feel and become curious about whatever comes up for you. And if nothing comes up for you, don't worry. Simply bring your attention back to your breath—breathing in and breathing out.

Imagine yourself five years from now. *Life is just as you had hoped. You have good health, financial security, and a beautiful family. You thoroughly enjoy how you're spending your days, and your relationships with friends and family are warm, supportive, and loving.*

Before opening your eyes in the morning, as you lie in bed, listen to the sounds that surround you. Perhaps you hear children's laughter, breaking waves in the distance, or the sounds of the city.

Notice the smells in the air—coffee brewing, fresh-cut grass, or salt air. What do you notice?

Now pay attention to the bedding that you're lying on. Does it feel crisp and clean? Is the fabric flannel, cotton, or silk? What does the space look like where you're sleeping?

Gently open your eyes and notice the colors of the room and of the linens.

If you're with someone, what does that being look like? Is it your pet? Your partner?

Describe what that being is like and the feelings that you hold for him or her.

Describe the details of the space and the furnishings.

How does it feel being in this room at this moment?

Walk over to the window and observe the outside. What do you notice—trees, mountains, cityscapes, gardens?

What time of year is it, and what is the climate like?

Walk into the bathroom and notice what this space looks like as you go through your morning rituals.

As you get dressed, put on whatever feels yummy and ideally suited for the day ahead.

Check yourself out in the mirror and notice the delight that you feel radiating health and vitality, knowing that today you look and feel great.

Okay, time for breakfast, coffee, or whatever delights you in the morning. Go into the kitchen area and picture what this part of your home looks like. All is set up just the way you like. Now imagine drinking a delicious cup of coffee or tea and savoring breakfast, eating anything that pleases you with everything arranged beautifully, and feeling relaxed yet excited about the day before you.

Is anyone with you, and if so, who are they? And what do you feel toward them?

How do they fit into your day?

What qualities do they have that bring you joy?

If something comes to mind that doesn't quite fit into this picture, no worries—just allow whatever comes to mind to surface. Allow it to pass through your mind like fair-weather clouds on a gloriously breezy, periwinkle blue-sky day.

Now you're ready to do whatever you would be doing in your ideal life. Remember, money is not an issue, so there are no financial demands to do anything in particular. You only do what matters in your heart of hearts. You feel a deep sense of satisfaction doing whatever it is you choose to do.

Perhaps you go into your home office and sit or stand at your computer, or you comfortably transport yourself to the place where you work.

Visualize where you work and what the feeling tone of this place is.

How are the pace and energy level of this place?

Do you feel engaged, inspired, connected?

Do you work alone, or with a partner or a team of people? If you work with others, who are they and how do these relationships feel to you?

Now, visualize what you are doing.

Are you helping others in need? If so, how are you doing this?

Are you writing or making something with your hands?

Are you solving problems that would make your work environment, your community, the world a better place?

Are you spending time with your family and friends, facilitating them in some way?

What do you imagine yourself doing? Whatever it is that you are doing, you know that you are making a difference for the greater good, which brings you solace and inner peace.

Picture now what you would do at midday.

Would you meet up with friends for lunch, or take a walk or jog through a beautiful park? Or perhaps you only work until lunch and return home to your family, volunteer somewhere, or pursue another interest such as yoga, horseback riding, or teaching English as a second language.

It's early evening now; imagine what you'd be doing and who you'd be meeting for dinner.

Are you home with family, with friends, at a dinner party, or are you gathering with a new group of people? You savor the delicious meal, the company, and the lovely energy, and afterward you begin to wind down.

You go through your evening rituals, readying yourself for bed, perhaps taking a leisurely bath and curling up in bed with a good book. You've had a wonderful day and you know that you're blessed to be living this life. The overriding feeling is deep gratitude as you drift off to sleep alone or with your partner.

When you're ready, slowly begin coming back to this moment and the life that you're living now, remembering the sweetness of this beautiful fantasy. Gradually, begin opening your eyes as you continue to breathe in and breathe out at your own pace.

Review

While your life may never look exactly like the one you visualized, going through this process is a window into the life you wish to create for yourself. It speaks to your heart's desire and your purpose in this beautiful and precious life of yours. You may wish to write down some of the thoughts, feelings, and images that came to mind. Visualizing and writing down what you wish to create in your life is often a precursor to the realization of those dreams and goals. In fact, it may be possible to start incorporating some of these experiences into your life right away.

This exercise is a wonderful way to remind yourself of the possibilities that lie before you. It can also help to restore your sense of hope and positivity when you're feeling bored, down, or disappointed in the way life is going. You can practice going through your ideal day whenever you need to rejuvenate or boost your energy level. You can extend and elaborate on this visualization or make it a quick fix, depending upon what will serve you best in the moment.

At different times you'll notice that you imagine different ideal days. After all, there are lots of wonderful ways to lead a day and a life. You might just find that giving yourself the opportunity to slip into this visualization helps you create more of these inspired, even magical, days in your life.

Whatever they may look like, when most of us string our ideal days together we discover our calling—which usually involves some form of being of service to others for the greater good. While we want to be the best that we can be, it's in our DNA to feel compassion for others and a desire to help them become more than who they have become. We naturally want to heal ourselves, the people in our lives, the environment, our communities, and the world.

I've heard it said that our life purpose is to lead a life of purpose. Perhaps one of your greatest purposes in life is to release this creative force that exists within you—like a sculptor chipping away the excess stone, so that the beauty inside can take shape.

Life purpose comes from insight, introspection, and life's lessons. We know what brings us joy and satisfaction—what makes us feel like our lives matter and that we make a difference for the greater good.

You're on this quest to improve your life—or you certainly would not be reading this book! You want more fullness, more richness, more vitality. No doubt, you want to wake up in the morning not only grateful for another day but also excited to live it out.

I strongly encourage you to wake up each day and practice your belly breaths and affirmation so that you create and live this beautiful new day to its fullest.

The 4:7:8 Breath

I'd like to introduce one more breathing exercise that I have not mentioned previously: the 4:7:8 breath. This breathing technique can be readily integrated into your day and takes about ninety seconds to practice.

When you find yourself worked up about something, anxious, or waking in the middle of the night, using this breath will quickly send a signal to your brain telling your mind and body to calm down.

Essentially, the idea is to breathe in to the count of four, hold your breath to the count of seven, and then purse your lips and breathe out slowly in a steady stream to the count of eight. This cycle is repeated four times and can be done whenever you wish to relax quickly or get back to sleep. Initially you may become a bit lightheaded from this exercise, but in time the sensation should feel quite pleasant.

It is not recommended that you practice more than four of these breaths consecutively. Four cycles of 4:7:8 breathing will be sufficient to induce a deep sense of relaxation. After several months of practice, if you wish to build up to eight cycles that's fine, but in all likelihood it won't be necessary. Also, never do this while driving. I recommend that you sit in a comfortable position or lie down in constructive-rest position when you first begin to practice the 4:7:8 breath.

Final Thoughts on Breathing

It's especially important to tune into and focus on your breathing whenever you catch yourself riddled with anxiety or stress, or when you find yourself unconsciously holding your breath. Conscious breathing taps you into your center and your power. It is your anchor and guide for life.

Although there are many takeaways within this book, if I were to narrow it down to a single idea, it's to remind you to return to a deepened breath whenever you find that you have strayed. This will always serve you well.

Daily Rituals to Support Your Best Life

The following is a series of rituals that will guide you throughout the day. They are meant to keep you on the path toward mind-body integration and create a foundation for discovering personal fulfillment.

Morning rituals:

- Belly breathe for two to three minutes.
- Brief meditation for five to ten minutes.
- Set positive intention for the day.

Afternoon rituals:

- Before lunch, two-minute belly breathing.
- As the day progresses, capture any negative thoughts. Get curious about what they mean to you. Reframe them in a way that is honest and more self-compassionate.
- Repeat daily positive intention as needed.

Evening rituals:

- Before dinner, practice two minutes of mindful breathing.
- Brief meditation for five to ten minutes to transition from day to evening.
- Moment of gratitude before dinner.

Nighttime rituals:

- Ideally, turn off all technology one hour before bed.
- Bathe, stretch, be intimate, or do some activity that helps you to unwind.
- Practice some belly breaths.
- Journal in bullet form aspects of the day for which you are grateful.
- If you have difficultly falling asleep or wake in the middle of the night, practice the 4:7:8 breath.

This is intended as a rough sketch for staying on track. You'll find that the length of time you spend on various activities changes with the needs and desires of your day. Your approach to homing in on the life you wish to lead may change over time. Regardless, these rituals or strategies will help provide structure for greater clarity, focus, and energy.

A Final Thought

While the strategies in *Behind the Therapy Door* are simple to learn, they can be challenging to maintain. I encourage you to seek reinforcement and updates through my website, www.DrRandyKamen. com, as well as my online courses, live retreats, and workshops. New information, webinars, and posts will be regularly added to the site so that you can receive ongoing support and inspiration on your path to greater mindfulness and fulfillment—so that you can travel well beyond the therapy door.

References

Chapter One

Mary Oliver, *New and Selected Poems, Volume One* (Boston: Beacon Hill Press, 1992).

Robert Putnam, *Bowling Alone: The Collapse and Revival of American Community* (New York: Simon & Schuster, 2000).

Michael Olpin and Margie Hesson, *Stress Management for Life: A Research-Based Experiential Approach* (Belmont, CA: Wadsworth Publishing, 2013).

Randy Kamen, *The Efficacy of Electromyographic Biofeedback in the Treatment of Chronic Low Back Pain* (Boston University, 1979).

Women's Health Study (WHS), "Women, Work, Stress, and Heart Disease: 5 Ways to Protect Yourself," *Harvard Health Publications,* Harvard Medical School (February 2011).

American Psychological Association, "Stress in America: Our Health at Risk," ed. Norman Anderson (2012).

Stanford Graduate School of Business, "The Psychology of Happiness," Case M-330 (August 2010).

Jon Kabat-Zinn, *Mindfulness for Beginners: Reclaiming the Present Moment—and Your Life* (Louisville, CO: Sounds True Inc., 2012).

Reed Larson, "Thirty Years of Research on the Subjective Well-Being of Older Americans," *The Journal of Gerontology* 33, no. 1 (1998).

Daniel Siegel, *Mindsight: The New Science of Personal Transformation* (New York: Bantam Books, 2011).

John Helliwell, Richard Layard, and Jeffrey Sachs (eds.), World Happiness Report, Earth Institute at Columbia University (2012).

Shelley E. Taylor, Laura C. Klein, Brian P. Lewis, Tara L. Gruenewald, Ragan A. R. Gurung, and John A. Updegraff, "Behavioral Responses to Stress: Tend and Befriend, Not Fight or Flight," *Psychological Review* 107, no. 3 (2002).

The Nurses' Health Study, Harvard Medical School (2013).

Ruthellen Josselson, *Best Friends: The Pleasure and Perils of Girls' and Women's Friendships* (New York: Crown Publishing Group, 1999).

Sarah Jane Glynn, "The New Breadwinners: 2010 Update: Rates of Women Supporting Their Families Economically Increased Since 2007," Center for American Progress (April 2012).

Betsey Stevenson and Justin Wolfers, "The Paradox of Declining Female Happiness," Federal Reserve Bank of San Francisco Working Paper Series, The Wharton School, University of Pennsylvania (2009–11).

Maria Shriver, "The Shriver Report: A Woman's Nation Changes Everything," eds. Heather Bushy and Ann O'Leary, Center for American Progress (October 2009).

Chapter Two

Herbert Benson and Miriam Klipper, *The Relaxation Response* (New York: HarperCollins, 1975).

George Valliant, *Spiritual Evolution: How We Are Wired for Faith, Hope, and Love* (New York: Broadway Books, 2008).

Jon Kabat-Zinn, *Wherever You Go, There You Are: Mindfulness Meditation in Everyday Life* (New York: Hyperion, 1994).

C. G. Jung, *Memories, Dreams, Reflections* (New York: Random House, 1961).

Martin Seligman, *Learned Optimism: How to Change Your Mind and Your Life* (New York: Simon & Schuster, 1998).

Daniel Taylor, *Tell Me a Story: The Life-Shaping Power of Our Stories* (St. Paul, MN: Bog Walk Press, 2005).

Chapter Three

Frank Hobbs and Nicole Stoops, "Demographic Trends in the 20th Century," *Census 2000 Special Reports* (November 2002).

Miller McPherson, Lynn Smith-Lovin, and Matthew Brashears, "Social Isolation in America: Changes in Core Discussion Networks over Two Decades," *American Sociological Review* 71, no. 3 (2006).

Martin Seligman, *Authentic Happiness: Using the New Positive Psychology to Realize Your Potential for Lasting Fulfillment* (New York: Simon & Schuster, 2002).

Robert Lane, "The Road Not Taken: Friendship, Consumerism, and Happiness," *Critical Review: A Journal of Politics and Society* 8, no. 4 (1994).

Beverly Fehr, "Friendship Processes," SAGE Series on Close Relationships, vol. 12. Sage Publications Inc. (1995).

Chapter Four

Peter Rudnytsky, ed., *Transitional Objects and Potential Spaces: Literary Uses of D. W. Winnicott* (New York: Columbia University Press, 1993).

Donald W. Winnicott, "Transitional Objects and Transitional Phenomena: A Study of the First Not-Me Possession," *International Journal of Psychoanalysis* (1953).

Donald W. Winnicott, "Mind and Its Relation to the Psyche-Soma," *British Journal of Medical Psychology* 27, no. 4 (September 1954).

Richard Davidson, with Sharon Begley, *The Emotional Life of Your Brain: How Its Unique Patterns Affect the Way You Think, Feel, and Live—and How You Can Change Them* (New York: Penguin, 2012).

Louise Hay, *Experience Your Good Now!: Learning to Use Affirmations* (Carlsbad, CA: Hay House, 2010).

Laura Kastner and Jennifer Wyatt, *Getting to Calm: Cool-Headed Strategies for Parenting Tweens + Teens* (Seattle: Ingram Publishing Services, 2009).

Mark Goulston, *Just Listen: Discover the Secret to Getting Through to Absolutely Anyone* (New York: AMACOM, 2010).

Foster Cline and Jim Fay, *Parenting Teens with Love and Logic: Preparing Adolescents for Responsible Adulthood, Updated and Expanded Edition* (Colorado Springs, CO: Pinon Press, 2006).

John Gottman and Nan Silver, *The Seven Principles for Making Marriage Work* (New York: Random House, 1999).

Chapter Five

Geneen Roth, *Breaking Free from Compulsive Eating* (London: Penguin Books, 1993).

Gershen Kaufman and Lev Raphael, *Dynamics of Power: Fighting Shame and Building Self-Esteem* (Rochester, VT: Schenkman Books, 1991).

Brené Brown, *Daring Greatly: How the Courage to Be Vulnerable Transforms the Way We Live, Love, Parent, and Lead* (New York: Penguin, 2012).

Brené Brown, *Men, Women, and Worthiness: The Experience of Shame and the Power of Being Enough* (Louisville, CO: Sounds True Publishing, 2013).

Thich Nhat Hanh and Lilian Cheung, *Savor: Mindful Eating, Mindful Life* (New York: HarperCollins, 2011).

Jan Chozen Bays, *Mindful Eating: A Guide to Rediscovering a Healthy and Joyful Relationship with Food* (Boston: Shambala Publishing, 2009).

Robert Enright, *Forgiveness Is a Choice: A Step-by-Step Process for Resolving Anger and Restoring Hope* (Washington, DC: American Psychological Association, 2001).

Lewis Smedes, *Forgive and Forget: Healing the Hurts We Don't Deserve* (New York: HarperCollins, 1996).

Teri Apter and Ruthellen Josselson, *Best Friends: The Pleasures and Perils of Girls' and Women's Friendships* (New York: Crown Publishing, Inc., 1998).

Chapter Six

American Cancer Society, Breast cancer statistics, http://www.cancer.org/cancer/breastcancer/detailedguide/breast-cancer-key-statistics

Gerald Epstein, *Healing Visualizations: Creating Health Through Imagery* (New York: Bantam Books, 1989).

Andrew Weil and Steven Gurgevich, *Heal Yourself with Medical Hypnosis: The Most Immediate Way to Use Your Mind-Body Connection* (Louisville, CO: Sounds True Publishing, 2005).

Susan G. Komen, Facts and resources for breast cancer, http://ww5.komen.org/Content.aspx?id=5692

Patricia San Pedro, Breast cancer resources and support, http://www.positivelypat.com

Susan Jeffers, *Feel the Fear and Do It Anyway* (Toronto: Random House, 1987).

Marc Silver, *Breast Cancer Husband: How to Help Your Wife (and Yourself) During Diagnosis, Treatment, and Beyond* (New York: Rodale, Inc., 2004).

Carolyn Kaelin, *Living Through Breast Cancer: What a Harvard Doctor and Survivor Wants You to Know About Getting the Best Care While Preserving Your Self-Image* (New York: McGraw-Hill, 2005).

Elisabeth Kübler-Ross, *On Grief and Grieving: Finding the Meaning of Grief Through the Five Stages of Loss* (New York: Scribner, 2005).

Chapter Seven

Sara M. Gorchoff, Oliver P. John, and Ravenna Helson, "Is Empty Nest Best? Changes in Marital Satisfaction in Late Middle Age," *Psychological Science* (November 2008).

Alzheimer's Association, http://www.alz.org/care/alzheimers-dementia-caregiver-stress-burnout.asp

Phakchok Rinpoche, *Keys to Happiness and a Meaningful Life* (Katmandu, Nepal: Lhasa Lotsawa Translations & Publications, 2012).

Richard Dawkins, *The Selfish Gene* (New York: Oxford University Press, 2006).

Stephen Post and Jill Neimark, *Why Good Things Happen to Good People* (New York: Broadway Books, 2007).

Jonathan Haidt, *The Happiness Hypothesis: Finding Modern Truth in Ancient Wisdom* (New York: Basic Books, 2006).

Nicholas Kristof and Sheryl WuDunn, *Half the Sky: Turning Oppression into Opportunity for Women Worldwide* (New York: Alfred A. Knopf, 2009).

Chapter Nine

Kristin Neff, *Self-Compassion: The Proven Power of Being Kind to Yourself* (New York: William Morrow Paperbacks, 2015).

Andrew Weil, *Breathing: The Master Key to Self Healing* (Louisville, CO: Sounds True Publishing, 1999).

Selected Bibliography

Anand, Margot, and J. P. Tarcher. *The Art of Sexual Ecstasy: The Path of Sacred Sexuality for Western Lovers* (New York: Penguin, 1989).

Apter, Teri, and Ruthellen Josselson. *Best Friends: The Pleasures and Perils of Girls' and Women's Friendships* (New York: Crown Publishing, 1998).

Beck, Martha. *Finding Your Way in a Wild New World: Reclaim Your True Nature to Create the Life You Want* (New York: Simon & Schuster, 2012).

Beck, Martha. *Steering by Starlight: Find Your Right Life, No Matter What!* (New York: Rodale, 2008).

Beck, Martha. *Finding Your Own North Star Journal: A Guide to Claiming the Life You Were Meant to Live* (New York: Crown Publishing, 2001).

Ben-Shahar, Tal. *Happier: Learn the Secrets to Daily Joy and Lasting Fulfillment* (New York: McGraw-Hill, 2005).

Benson, Herbert, and Miriam Klipper. *The Relaxation Response* (New York: HarperCollins, 1975).

Borysenko, Joan. *Minding the Body, Mending the Mind* (Cambridge, MA: Perseus Books, 2007).

Brach, Tara. *Radical Acceptance: Embracing Your Life with the Heart of a Buddha* (New York: Random House, 2003).

Burns, David. *The Feeling Good Handbook* (New York: Penguin, 1999).

Chödrön, Pema. *When Things Fall Apart: Heart Advice for Difficult Times* (Boston: Shambala Publications, 1997).

Chopra, Deepak. *Perfect Health: The Complete Mind/Body Guide, Revised and Updated Edition* (New York: Crown Publishing, 2000).

Chopra, Deepak. *The Seven Spiritual Laws of Success: A Practical Guide to the Fulfillment of Your Dreams* (San Rafael, CA: Amber-Allan Publishing, 1994).

Chopra, Deepak, and David Simon. *The Seven Spiritual Laws of Yoga: A Practical Guide to Healing Body, Mind, and Spirit* (Hoboken, NJ: John Wiley & Sons, 2004).

Chopra, Deepak. *The Ultimate Happiness Prescription: 7 Keys to Joy and Enlightenment* (New York: Random House, 2009).

Cline, Elizabeth. *Overdressed: The Shockingly High Cost of Cheap Fashion* (New York: Penguin, 2012).

Cohen, Carolyn Joy. *A Blessing in Disguise: 39 File Lessons from Today's Greatest Teachers* (New York: Penguin, 2008).

Csikszentmihályi, Mihály. *Flow: The Psychology of Optimal Experience* (New York: HarperCollins, 1990).

Dalai Lama. *How to Be Compassionate: A Handbook for Creating Inner Peace and a Happier World* (New York: Simon & Schuster, 2011).

Dalai Lama. *The Art of Happiness: A Handbook for Living* (New York: Penguin, 2009).

Deits, Bob. *Life After Loss: A Practical Guide to Renewing Your Life After Experiencing Major Loss* (Cambridge, MA: Perseus, 2009).

Domar, Alice, and Henry Dreher. *Self-Nurture: Learning to Care for Yourself as Effectively as You Care for Everyone Else* (New York: Penguin, 2001).

Frankl, Viktor. *Man's Search for Meaning* (Boston: Beacon Press, 2006).

Fredrickson, Barbara. *Positivity: Groundbreaking Research Reveals How to Embrace the Hidden Strength of Positive Emotions, Overcome Negativity, and Thrive* (New York: Random House, 2009).

Gilbert, Daniel. *Stumbling on Happiness* (New York: Random House, 2005).

Gilligan, Carol. *In a Different Voice: Psychological Theory and Women's Development* (Cambridge, MA: Harvard University Press, 1982).

Goleman, Daniel. *Emotional Intelligence: Why It Can Matter More Than IQ* (New York: Bantam, 1995).

Goleman, Daniel. *Social Intelligence: The New Science of Human Relationships* (New York: Random House, 2006).

Gottman, John, and Nan Silver. *The Seven Principles for Making Marriage Work* (New York: Random House, 1999).

Graf von Dürckheim, Karlfried. *The Way of Transformation: Daily Life as Spiritual Practice* (Sandpoint, ID: Morning Light Press, 2007).

Gross, Jane. *A Bittersweet Season: Caring for Our Aging Parents—and Ourselves* (New York: Random House, 2012).

Hanson, Rick. *Buddha's Brain: The Practical Neuroscience of Happiness, Love, and Wisdom* (Oakland, CA: New Harbinger Publications, 2009).

Hendricks, Gay. *Conscious Breathing: Breathwork for Health, Stress Release, and Personal Mastery* (New York: Random House, 1995).

Hendrix, Harville. *Getting the Love You Want: A Guide for Couples* (New York: Henry Holt and Company, 1988, 2008).

Johnson, Sue. *Hold Me Tight: Seven Conversations for a Lifetime of Love* (New York: Little, Brown and Company, 2008).

Josselson, Ruthellen. *Best Friends: The Pleasure and Perils of Girls' and Women's Friendships* (New York: Crown Publishing, 1999).

Jung, Carl. *Memories, Dreams, Reflections* (New York: Random House, 1961).

Kabat-Zinn, Myla, and Jon Kabat-Zinn. *Everyday Blessings: The Inner Work of Mindful Parenting* (New York: Hyperion, 1997).

Kabat-Zinn, Jon. *Full Catastrophic Living: Using the Wisdom of Your Body and Mind to Face Stress, Pain, and Illness* (New York: Random House, 2005).

Kabat-Zinn, Jon. *Mindfulness for Beginners: Reclaiming the Present Moment—and Your Life* (Louisville, CO: Sounds True Inc., 2012).

Kabat-Zinn, Jon. *Wherever You Go, There You Are: Mindfulness Meditation in Everyday Life* (New York: Hyperion, 1994).

Kristof, Nicholas, and Sheryl WuDunn. *Half the Sky: Turning Oppression into Opportunity for Women Worldwide* (New York: Random House, 2010).

Kübler-Ross, Elisabeth. *On Death and Dying: What the Dying Have to Teach Doctors, Nurses, Clergy and Their Own Families* (New York: Simon & Schuster, 1997).

Kübler-Ross, Elisabeth. *On Grief and Grieving: Finding the Meaning of Grief Through the Five Stages of Loss* (New York: Scribner, 2005).

Kushner, Harold. *When Bad Things Happen to Good People* (New York: Random House, 1989).

Lerner, Harriet. *The Dance of Anger: A Woman's Guide to Changing the Patterns of Intimate Relationships* (New York: HarperCollins, 2005).

Lerner, Harriet. *The Dance of Intimacy: A Woman's Guide to Courageous Acts of Change in Key Relationships* (New York: Harper & Row, 1990).

Lesser, Elizabeth. *Broken Open: How Difficult Times Can Help Us Grow* (New York: Random House, 2005).

Lessing, Doris. *The Golden Notebook* (New York: Simon & Schuster, 1962).

Luskin, Fred. *Forgive for Good: A Proven Prescription for Health and Happiness* (New York: HarperCollins, 2002).

Lyubomirsky, Sonja. *The How of Happiness: A Scientific Approach to Getting the Life You Want* (New York: Penguin, 2007).

Miller, Jean Baker, and Irene Pierce Stiver. *The Healing Connection: How Women Form Relationships in Therapy and in Life* (Boston: Beacon Press, 1997).

Mortenson, Greg, and David Oliver Relin. *Three Cups of Tea: One Man's Mission to Promote Peace . . . One School at a Time* (New York: Penguin, 2009).

Myss, Caroline. *Why People Don't Heal and How They Can* (New York: Crown Publishing Group, 1997).

Nhat Hanh, Thich. *Being Peace* (Berkeley, CA: Parallax Press, 2005).

Nhat Hanh, Thich. *Peace Is Every Breath: A Practice for Our Busy Lives* (New York: HarperCollins, 2011).

Nhat Hanh, Thich. *Peace Is Every Step: The Path of Mindfulness in Everyday Life* (New York: Bantam Books, 1991).

Nhat Hanh, Thich. *Taming the Tiger Within: Meditations on Transforming Difficult Emotions* (New York: Penguin, 2004).

Northrop, Christiane. *Women's Bodies, Women's Wisdom; Creating Physical and Emotional Health and Healing* (New York: Bantam Books, 1998).

Ornish, Dean. *Love and Survival: The Scientific Basis for the Healing Power of Intimacy* (New York: HarperCollins, 1998).

Putnam, Robert. *Bowling Alone: The Collapse and Revival of American Community* (New York: Simon & Schuster, 2000).

Ram Dass, and Mirabai Bush. *Compassion in Action: Setting Out on the Path of Service* (New York: HarperCollins, 1992).

Ram Dass. *Remember, Be Here Now* (New York: Crown Publishing, 1971).

Ram Dass. *The Only Dance There Is* (New York: Random House, 1974).

Real, Terrence. *The New Rules of Marriage: What You Need to Know to Make Love Work* (New York: Random House, 2008).

Remen, Rachel Naomi. *Kitchen Table Wisdom: Stories That Heal* (New York: Penguin, 2006).

Rinpoche, Sogyal. *The Tibetan Book of Living and Dying* (New York: HarperCollins, 2002).

Rubin, Gretchen. *The Happiness Project: Or, Why I Spent a Year Trying to Sing in the Morning, Clean My Closets, Fight Right, Read Aristotle, and Generally Have More Fun* (New York: HarperCollins, 2009).

Salzberg, Sharon. *Lovingkindness: The Revolutionary Art of Happiness* (Boston: Shambala Publications, 1995).

Salzberg, Sharon. *Real Happiness: The Power of Meditation* (New York: Workman Publishing Company, 2011).

Salzberg, Sharon, and Mirabai Bush. *Voices of Insight* (Boston: Shambala Publications, 2001).

Sandberg, Cheryl. *Lean In: Women, Work, and the Will to Lead* (New York: Random House, 2013).

Seligman, Martin. *Authentic Happiness: Using the New Positive Psychology to Realize Your Potential for Lasting Fulfillment* (New York: Simon & Schuster, 2002).

Selye, Hans. *Stress Without Distress* (Philadelphia: J. B. Lippincott, 1974).

Selye, Hans. *The Stress of Life* (New York: McGraw-Hill, 1956).

Shimoff, Marci. *Happy for No Reason: 7 Steps to Being Happy from the Inside Out* (New York: Simon & Schuster, 2008).

Siegel, Daniel. *Mindsight: The New Science of Personal Transformation* (New York: Bantam Books, 2011).

Siegel, Daniel. *The Mindful Brain: Reflection and Attunement in the Cultivation of Well-Being* (New York: W. W. Norton & Company, 2007).

Steinem, Gloria. *A Book of Self-Esteem: Revolution from Within* (Boston: Little, Brown & Company, 1993).

Taylor, S. E., L. C. Klein, B. P. Lewis, T. L. Gruenewald, R. A. R. Gurung, and J. A. Updegraff, "Behavioral Responses to Stress: Tend and Befriend, Not Fight or Flight," *Psychological Review*, 107, no. 3: July 2000, 411–29.

Toffler, Alvin. *Future Shock* (New York: Random House, 1970).

Tolle, Eckhart. *The Power of Now: A Guide to Spiritual Enlightenment* (Novato, CA: New World Library, 1999).

Weil, Andrew. *Spontaneous Happiness* (New York: Little, Brown & Company, 2011).

Weil, Andrew. *Spontaneous Healing: How to Discover and Embrace Your Body's Natural Ability to Maintain and Heal Itself* (New York: Random House, 1995).

Williamson, Marianne. *The Age of Miracles: Embracing the New Midlife* (Carlsbad, CA: Hay House, 2008).

Williamson, Marianne. *The Law of Divine Compensation: On Work, Money, and Miracles* (New York: HarperCollins, 2012).